# UNDER A FIG TREE

# UNDER A FIG TREE

*A Family Memoir*

Sandra M. Levesque

The poem, "Black Dresses," used by permission,
is from *Italian Women in Black Dresses*, by Maria Mazziotti Gillan,
published by Guernica Editions, Inc., Toronto, Ontario, Canada.
First edition printing, November 2002.

Map design:
Ronald F. Varga, Muskegon, MI

Book and cover design:
Karen Thorkilsen, East Barnard, VT
www.karenthorkilsen.com

Contemporary photographs of
Sicily; Rutland, Vermont; the Statue of Liberty; and Ellis Island
by Sandra M. Levesque.

© August 2009. Second Printing, December 2009.
Sandra M. Levesque
100 Gilead Brook Road
Randolph, VT 05060
sandylev@together.net

All rights reserved.

ISBN: 1-4486-5561-7
EAN–13: 978-1-4486-5561-8

*Dedicated to*
*the Scafidi Sisters*
*Venera, Concetta, Maria, and Assunta*


*For*
*Rhaine, Tully, Alexander, and Cassandra*

## CONTENTS

|  | Acknowledgments | ix |
|---|---|---|
|  | Prologue: The Last Explanation | 1 |
| I | The Stories | 5 |
| II | Francesco Paolo | 11 |
| III | Antonia & Francesco Paolo | 21 |
| IV | The Crossing | 25 |
| V | Ellis Island Then | 31 |
| VI | Ellis Island Today | 37 |
| VII | Randazzo to Rutland | 43 |
| VIII | Return to Randazzo | 51 |
| IX | Finding Francesco Paolo | 59 |
| X | Discovering Antonia's World | 69 |
| XI | The Delpopolos | 75 |
| XII | I Remember Nana | 87 |
| XIII | The Neighborhood | 97 |
| XIV | Our Church | 109 |
| XV | The Sisters of St. Joseph | 121 |
| XVI | Our Daily Bread | 129 |
| XVII | Nana's Cucina | 143 |
| XVIII | Making A Living…Making A Life | 161 |
| XIX | Societa' Sicula Americana | 175 |
| XX | The Scafidi Sisters | 183 |
|  | Epilogue | 211 |
|  | The Family Genealogy | 215 |

# ACKNOWLEDGMENTS

A family memoir is a collaboration, particularly if you are fortunate, as I have been, to engage the previous generation of family oracles. Maria Concetta Miglis, "Aunt Jata," was the High Priestess of Storytelling in our family. She died at 86, just weeks before the publication of this book. Without her remarkable recall of detail in countless hours of interview, her characteristic generosity in sharing recipes, letters, and photographs, and her boundless enthusiasm for the project, I may not have been able to assemble this 1,000-piece puzzle. We remembered together and celebrated each revelation in an endless conversation that spanned three years. She is missed.

Concetta's sister, Mary Valleroli, is the last Keeper of Stories from our family's first generation of Italian-Americans. She, too, enriched the project with loving and intimate recollections of her parents, sisters, and a way of life that now challenges the imagination.

Other family members of the next generation made significant contributions. Ron Varga created the maps. Michele Cioffi, Judy Lamberti, Joanne Louras, and Charron Valleroli shared photographs and documents. Susan Brock was a manuscript reviewer.

Marcia Folsom, Stephen Morris, and Christopher Costanzo also gave their time generously to review the manuscript. How lucky to have Chris, an Italian scholar, as my neighbor and friend. His willingness to translate family papers and letters that surfaced during the research process provided fresh insight and helped to unravel the story from the "other side."

There were also helpers across the Atlantic – Matteo Ferretti, my welcoming host in Randazzo; Tony Sparta from the Randazzo Tourist Bureau, the Sicilian Pied Piper who led me through the winding streets of my grandfather's hometown; and Ernest Natividad, a family friend living in Sicily who took me behind the scenes in Catania with his flawless command of the language.

Back in Vermont, Jim Davidson, my high school American History teacher and the driving force behind the Rutland Historical Society, proved to be a dogged researcher and an eager accomplice in sleuthing through the society's well-organized archives. Paul Carnahan, Head

Librarian of the Vermont Historical Society, briskly walked me through the maze of genealogy formatting. I am grateful to both.

Garrison Keillor, through a writing workshop that inspired the project, helped me find my voice as the family narrator. My partner, Stephen Morris, shared every step of the journey that followed with unflagging interest in my work and enormous consideration for the time I devoted to it. Who else would understand a vacation in Puerto Rico devoted to finishing the manuscript?

Karen Thorkilsen is the book designer who shares my sense of aesthetics and breathed beauty into the pages that follow.

True to form, my children, Stephen and Heather Levesque, have been front row cheerleaders.

To them, and to all of the generous supporters I encountered from Sicily to Ellis Island to Rutland, Vermont, I extend my gratitude for the part they have played in bringing these stories and images to the printed page.

# UNDER A FIG TREE

*A Scafidi family portrait from 1931.*
*Back row: Venera, Francesco, and Antonia.*
*Front row: Maria, Assunta, and Concetta.*

# PROLOGUE
# THE LAST EXPLANATION

*Cu' ad autru 'nzigna, acquista cchiu sapiri.*
WHO TEACHES ANOTHER, ACQUIRES MORE KNOWLEDGE.

When grandparents die, the last explanation goes with them. Nearly 40 years have passed since my maternal grandmother, Antonia Maria Delpopolo Scafidi, left us with the indelible spirit of a life that her children and grandchildren love and strive to remember.

I am twice removed from her story. Time has diluted the thin details of what she and my grandfather chose to share, and the whole truths were never really accessible. Perhaps it was too painful for them to remember who and what they left behind in Sicily, to say nothing of how they carved out new lives an ocean away. For their children, my mother and her three sisters, first generation Americans trying to assimilate to a culture in conflict with that of their parents, it may have been easier to forget.

Or, it may be the "vertiginous" tradition of Sicily, "the secret island," as Giuseppe DiLampedusa described his homeland in the classic historical novel, *The Leopard*. This is a place "where, in an ostentatious show of mystery, houses are barred and peasants refuse to admit they even know the way to their own village in clear view on a hillock within a few miles walk."

*Under a Fig Tree* started at my grandmother's kitchen table when I was old enough to be curious and young enough to be trusted with secrets, which are hard to have and to hold at any age. The family memoir is my attempt to retell the stories pried from this reticent woman with the added perspective of historical research. Her daughters' first-hand accounts of growing up with Mama and Papa in the pre- and post-

Depression years of their childhoods add the color vision. Interspersed are personal recollections, snapshots of a fading time and place.

The photographs and documents my grandparents brought with them peel back more layers, filling in long-standing blanks in the family narrative and providing a few surprises, as well. My first visit to Sicily in August 1997, and the research trip to my grandparents' "hometowns" of Randazzo and Castiglione di Sicilia that followed in October 2007, gave me authentic, first-hand experience to become a believable storyteller.

I returned from my last trip with a new twist on our family's old story, quite different from the hand-me-down interpretation of my grandparents' lives. For me, the worn threads of melancholia, loss, and struggle faded when I began to appreciate the rich tapestry of their daring and transforming experience as part of the largest human migration in modern history. I believe that my grandparents did realize the American dream. They also suffered hard realities unimaginable in their youth.

But the complete story of their lives, the last explanation, was buried with them and all of the other first generation immigrants who truly experienced the "old country" in full nuance. The women passed along the secrets of *la cucina* to their daughters and to their sons' wives. The men formed closed societies that perpetuated the Sicilian sense of localism with secretive meetings of the brotherhood. Together they celebrated the feast days of their Sicilian villages' patron saints with annual festivals, familiar food, and pageantry. They named their children in honor of those left behind, without any explanation or resistance as immigration officers, parish priests, doctors, and teachers Anglicized their first and family names.

Regardless, in their new world they fiercely protected their identity as *Siciliani* first and Italians second. They were the dominant forces in their communities, adhering to the social life, entrenched eating habits, and rituals of their villages. Their children, the transition generation faced with bridging both ways of life, were called Italian-Americans, albeit more Italian than American. They knew little of life in the old country, which made it easier for them to let go of their parents' customs and connections. The Italian-American ratio eventually reversed itself as their descendants melted into the great American society, fully adopting a new way of life.

It seems that every Italian girl has a story about Nana.* This is mine.

*The correct dialectical spelling of grandmother is Nanna, as is Nannu for grandfather. There is a tendency in many Italian-American families, including ours, to de-emphasize the double consonant, which is why I use the familiar Nana and Nanu throughout this memoir.*

*Castiglione di Sicilia, birthplace of Antonia Maria Delpopolo Scafidi, October 2007.*

# CHAPTER I
# THE STORIES

*Chiddu ch'e scrittu, leggiri si voli.*
THAT WHICH IS WRITTEN, IS MEANT TO BE READ.

## ANTONIA

As the 20th century dawned in Castiglione di Sicilia, Italy, Antonia Spucches could often be found entertaining her first granddaughter and namesake, Antonia Maria Delpopolo, with wondrous stories of kings, queens and palaces. Antonia Maria's favorite fairytale, which she later told to her daughters in America, was about another little girl who received an unexpected invitation to the King's Ball. The Sicilian Cinderella danced the night away in pretty blue shoes, on floors made of gold bars. As the young girl's slippers swept across the surface, they picked up particles of gold, which she eagerly brought home to her poor parents. From that evening on, the girl lived as happily as a princess in her village.

The roots of this folktale are imbedded in Sicily's feudal past when, in contrast to the rich abundance of those who ruled over them, the island's peasantry lived in unimaginable poverty with scarcity the norm. The Sicily of my grandmother's youth was still a land of hardscrabble subsistence with limited horizons, particularly for its native daughters. Countrywomen did not go to school for long, if at all. Most were sent to the fields and vineyards, where they worked alongside, and as hard as, men. They were also expected to help their mothers with wood gathering, bread making, laundry, cheese and soap making until it was time for them to marry, raise children and nurse their own families and elderly parents through difficult times.

Antonia Maria was 22 years old when she accepted a proposal of marriage from Francesco Paolo Scafidi, an adventurous man of the world, ten years her senior, who told her he would take her to America. In accepting his hand and his promise, Antonia may have shared the immigrant's dream of streets paved with gold, an image closer to the fairytale of her early childhood than the glaring reality and dim prospects of her village life.

Implicit in Antonia's marriage contract was leaving, for the first time, the only home she had ever known. I cannot imagine that the young, sheltered woman parted from her family fully comprehending that she would never see them, or Sicily, again. For the rest of her life, she sadly recalled her final encounter with her father, Salvatore, who insisted on accompanying his eldest daughter and her new husband to the train station that commenced their long trip to Ellis Island. Antonia and Francesco Paolo were bound first for Palermo, where they were to board an immigrant ship for the Atlantic crossing. As the train pulled away from the station, Antonia locked eyes with her father, who stood alone by the rail. The image seared in her memory was of her father's fedora being blown off his head by a gust of wind as he waved them out of sight. He probably did not know that Antonia was three months pregnant with her first child, my mother. It was August 1920.

## UNDER A FIG TREE

> *Who can find a good woman?*
> *She is precious beyond all things.*
> *Her husband's heart trusts her completely.*
> *She is his best reward.*
>
> *Proverbs 31: 10-11*

My grandfather was discharged from a cavalry unit of the Italian Army in July 1919 and returned to his hometown of Randazzo where he owned a house and land. It would not have been unusual for all able-bodied men in the grape-growing region to be pressed into service in nearby villages during the harvest. Randazzo was just nine miles from the village where Antonia and her family lived.

*From the collection of Christopher Costanzo, an 1821 painting of a young Sicilian woman from the Mt. Etna region.*

When questioned about her past, my grandmother, Nana, allowed that she came from Catania, where she and my grandfather met, *nelle vigne all ombra del fico,* under the shade of a fig tree. Along with her mother and three sisters, she made and delivered bread to the men working in the vineyards, as part of their mid-day meal. A shady fig tree in an open stretch of grape-growing fields would offer welcome relief from the scorching Sicilian sun at high noon.

While my grandmother always referred to Catania as her home in Sicily, the village of Castiglione di Sicilia, as well as Randazzo, are among the fifty-eight towns and cities that comprise the Regional Province of Catania. In Sicily, as in all of Italy, identification with *paesi*, provinces, is an important and often overarching association.

As a young girl, I remember feeling part of a happy conspiracy when Nana showed me the muslin cloth that she wrapped around her neck and shoulders to create a sling-like pouch for transporting loaves of bread, the basic food of Sicily's hard-working peasants. The cloth could also be coiled and wrapped around her head to support a basket with the rest of the meal's staples: fruit, cheese, and salami, or a jug of water, that she called *acqua terra*.

It was hard for me to believe that the ample woman swaying across the kitchen, hands on hips, demonstrating how the basket was balanced on the way to the vineyards, was my usually reserved grandmother. That long piece of muslin was packed with homemade dowry linens, clothing, and household items in one of two steamer trunks she was allowed to take on board the New York, U.S.A. bound ship from Palermo.

While Nana's explanation of how she and my grandfather met seemed simple, it also offered a glimpse of the prevailing Sicilian culture. The agro-workplace provided social opportunities for young people from neighboring, but isolated, villages to become acquainted. At the end of the day, vineyard laborers gathered around campfires in the closest village for an evening of song, dance, and storytelling. Some of the men played accordion and mandolin, while the women sewed, made lace, or worked on their fine embroidery, the hallmark handcraft of Castiglione di Sicilia. In the case of my grandparents, it was Nana's father who owned the small vineyard where Francesco Paolo was employed as a day laborer.

Antonia and Francesco Paolo never dated. The closest approximation came during their pre-engagement period when they sat directly across from one another at the evening campfires. Since they married on March 25, 1920, Francesco and Antonia probably met sometime during the grape harvest in the fall of 1919, which made for an engagement period of four to six months.

*During World War I, Corporal Francesco Paolo Scafidi served in the Italian Cavalry from 1916 to 1919.*

## CHAPTER II
## FRANCESCO PAOLO

*Italia Redenta ed Una, Per Valore dei Suoi Soldati*
ITALY, REDEEMED AND ONE, THROUGH THE BRAVERY OF ITS SOLDIERS

I started out to write my grandmother's story, which seemed destined to recede into the past. In the process, I discovered my much better documented grandfather, who we called Nanu. Immigration papers, family correspondence, military records, house deeds, and the skeleton of a work history helped recreate Francesco Paolo, the aloof Frank Scafidi of my youth.

My grandfather thought that girls, including his daughters, should be quiet and listen, speaking only when spoken to—an attitude that did not engender the close kind of relationship that I enjoyed with my grandmother. He looms in my memory as a proud, stern man, who forever maintained a dignified bearing.

Not long after his 25th birthday in 1913, he made his way from Randazzo to Palermo, where he boarded the ship, *Re D Italia*, bound for the United States. Word had spread from the Italian peninsula to down-on-its-heels Sicily that unheard of opportunities existed in America. It was common for young men to follow the promise of good paying jobs across the Atlantic, often returning to their homelands with saved wages and an elevated status. According to information provided by Ellis Island, one-third of all immigrants who passed through the processing center traveled back and forth before finally deciding to stay in the old country or to settle permanently in the United States. The practice was so common among Italian men that the term "birds of passage" was used to describe those who intentionally planned a temporary stay to improve their lot.

Francesco Paolo traveled alone, reaching the port of New York City on February 28, 1913, in the middle of winter in the northeastern U.S. The young man, who had seen Mt. Etna's six month snow-cap from a distance and, perhaps, experienced an occasional light snowfall in his hometown, continued his journey north to one of the coldest and snowiest states in the country, Vermont.

Five to six years prior to his arrival, fellow immigrants from Randazzo had begun to establish a community in Rutland. During this period of mass migration from Sicily, fellow villagers often emigrated and re-settled together in areas with abundant employment opportunities. Francesco Paolo found room and board with the Rocco Cioffi family on West Street, close to Rutland's downtown area.

The next year, on May 10, 1914, Salvatore Scafidi, Francesco Paolo's older brother by four years, arrived at Ellis Island aboard the ship, *Palermo*, from the port of Naples. Salvatore, who was 30 years old at the time, may have initially left Sicily to find work on the Italian mainland, which might explain his departure from Naples. Upon arriving in the United States, he traveled to Rutland, where he was reunited with his younger brother, Francesco Paolo—albeit not for long.

With the outbreak of World War I, the younger Scafidi man was called back to Sicily to join the Italian army under the leadership of King Umberto I. Although not an eager recruit, Francesco Paolo departed from New York in September 1915, just two and one-half years after his arrival. Had he not responded to the call, he would have been barred from re-entering Sicily for the next 20 years. The property he owned in Randazzo might have been in jeopardy had he remained in the United States and he would have been involuntarily separated from his parents and extended family still in Sicily.

My grandfather's military records indicate that he joined the Italian Cavalry on July 19, 1916. Following three years of meritorious service, Corporal Scafidi was honorably discharged on July 12, 1919. The cavalry

*The Savio Calvary Regiment of the Italian Army.
Corporal Scafidi (second from left in the second row) is holding a proclamation.*

*The Savio Calvary Regiment was stationed in Torino, Italy.
Corporal Scafidi is standing proud, with hand on hip, second from the left in the back row.*

saw action in Italy, Austria, and Germany. Francesco Paolo's unit, the Savio Calvary Regiment, was stationed in Torino, a northern Italian city in the Piedmont Region. His discharge papers granted him an unlimited leave and permission to return to Randazzo, in the military district of Acireale. He was required to "present himself to the local command" of the *carbinieri*, rural Sicily's powerful police force.

Francesco Paolo carried two keepsakes from his military service to America—a black leather riding crop, his *frustino*, and a commemorative red and cream-colored neckerchief, imprinted with the map of Italy and the inscription, *ITALIA REDENTA ED UNA, Per Valore dei Suoi Soldati, 3 Novembre 1918*—"Italy, Redeemed and One, Through the Bravery of Its Soldiers, November 3, 1918."

With saved wages from Vermont and military pay in his pocket, Francesco Paolo faced his upcoming 32nd birthday with an urgency to get on with life. His brother, Salvatore, was waiting for him in Vermont with a community of friends and the promise of a good paying job. The next order of business would be to find a wife with whom he could return to America and start a family. That is exactly what happened within a matter of months.

Francesco Paolo Scafidi was 32 years old and, relative to the time and the place, a man of some means when he married my grandmother. He had enough money to fulfill the social contract of outfitting his wife in gold jewelry, both as a wedding gift and as proof that he could support a family. He was able to arrange a wedding portrait and book passage to America for himself and his bride—no small feat. At a time when you supposedly could eat for one week on one lire, the cost of a *posti di 3rd classe*—a third class ticket to America—was 700 lire! That was the U.S. equivalent of $35.00, so the 1,400 lire that my grandfather paid for two tickets, in addition to all of the other travel expenses associated with the trip, added up to an impressive sum.

Francesco Paolo's stance in photographs and his style of dress indicate that he was a dapper man, later confirmed during my research in Randazzo. In one of the early photographs taken after his arrival in the U.S., my grandfather and Luigi Cala, a friend from Randazzo with whom he jointly purchased a house in Rutland, are wearing matching plaid hats—a sign, I was told, that they traded their standard-issue black felt Sicilian caps (still in fashion today) for modern American fashion.

*Francesco Paolo Scafidi and his good friend from Randazzo, Luigi Cala, pose for a studio photograph in their new "American" caps. Less than four years after their emigration, Francesco and Luigi jointly purchased a large, two-family house in the heart of Rutland's Italian neighborhood. Luigi and his sister, Carmella Cala Rotella, were the Baptismal sponsors (Godfather and Godmother) for the Scafidi couple's first-born child, Venera. During my research trip to Randazzo in 2007, I serendipitously encountered one of Luigi Cala's relatives at a municipal office, where he applied for a permit to forage Etna mushrooms. He strongly resembled the young Luigi in the photograph I had with me—and he was wearing the traditional black Sicilian cap.*

*Francesco Paolo*

For the rest of his life, my grandfather was rarely without a stylish hat—felt fedoras and straw brimmed boaters—always the natty dresser. He wore buttoned cardigan sweaters year-round and tightly seamed dress pants that he pressed between the mattress and box spring of his bed. In warm weather months, he kept mint leaves in his pockets, so that he could rub the leaves together as he walked, releasing the herb's fresh fragrance.

Nanu's family, like so many other Sicilian families of his time, lived in the tight quarters of an ancient village, but worked in the *campagna*—the countryside—where they owned land with gardens, vineyards, and orchards. Family correspondence indicates that my grandfather left property behind in, or around, Randazzo when he immigrated to America. I suspect that he intended to return someday, since he allowed his nephews in Randazzo to use the land and to keep the profits from whatever they produced, but would not give in to their written requests to transfer ownership. The unclear disposition of the land eventually gave rise to a family feud.

In 1957, my grandfather received a letter from one of his nephews, Vincenzo Scafidi, who made reference to 20 years of saved correspondence and a 10-year, unresolved legal case regarding the property, petitioning his uncle to end the dispute and grant him, "the true heir of the Scafidi family," ownership. The dispute in question was between Vincenzo, the son of my grandfather's older brother, Salvatore, and Salvatore Manitta, who married Alfia Scafidi, the daughter of my grandfather's brother, Antonio. In a stroke of Sicilian temper, Vincenzo wrote that Salvatore Manitta was "the most foolish among the husbands of my cousins and the most evil."

My grandfather made no attempt to resolve the conflict in his lifetime, nor have any of his descendants in the fifty-one years since his death. My field research in Randazzo suggests that the land in question lies east of the city, where the vineyards begin to dominate a landscape of lava rock terraces and walls, dwarfed by Mt. Etna. This is also the direction that my grandfather's brother, Salvatore, took when he returned to Randazzo to marry Arfia Bordonaro, following his 10-year stint in Vermont. Soon after their wedding, he bought his bride a house in Montelaguardia, an easy three-mile walk from his hometown.

*Vincenzo and Angela Scafidi
on their wedding day in Randazzo, Sicily.*

*Salvatore Manitta served in the Italian
Army during World War II.*

*Salvatore and Arfia Scafidi,
the sister of Gaetana Foti,
who emigrated from Randazzo to Rutland,
Vermont with her husband Giuseppe.*

*Mr. and Mrs. Antonio Scafidi*

*Wedding photograph of Francesco Paolo and Antonia Maria Delpopolo Scafidi, 1920.*

# CHAPTER III
# ANTONIA & FRANCESCO PAOLO

*Amuri, tutti dicinu ch'e amaru, e ognunu voli pruvari siddu e veru.*
LOVE, EVERYONE SAYS IT'S BITTER,
BUT EVERYONE WANTS TO SEE FOR THEMSELVES IF IT'S TRUE.

My grandparents' *Certificato di Matrimonio* was issued in Castiglione di Sicilia, where they were married in one of the village churches on March 5, 1920. The Mother Church is dedicated to Saint Peter, but the Castiglione is also home to three others: the Church of the Benedictine Sisters, the church of Sant' Antonio, and the 16th-century church of the Madonna della Catena. While the couple's union was officially recognized by the civil state of Sicily, the Vatican imposed a nine-year waiting period before validating the marriage—as was the custom with all Catholic marriages in Italy at that time.

In my grandparents' wedding photo, Antonia is wearing a green velvet dress with a laced trimmed bodice, perhaps lace that she or a family member made for the special occasion. My grandfather is fashionably dressed in a black suit and tie, with a gold watch fob on his lapel.

It would not have been unusual for Antonia to literally leave her family on the day of her marriage, and to spend her wedding night in Randazzo, at Fracesco Paolo's house, or that of his parents. Her passport, which was issued on May 22, 1920, indicates that she was a resident of Randazzo at that time of application.

Antonia is wearing her wedding dress in the passport photo. She is described as being 1.55 meters (5' 1.5") in height, svelte, with a low forehead, and chestnut hair. "Brown" is listed for her color, as is

Francesco's on his passport. He is also photographed in his wedding finery, and described as being 1.64 meters (5'5") in height, of regular body weight, with a high forehead, chestnut hair, and a trimmed moustache.

Their passports were issued for emigration purposes only, in the name of Vittorio Emanuele III, Italy's then constitutional monarch. The legal terms of these special passports required that the bearers leave Sicily no later than December 30, 1920, on an officially designated immigrant ship destined for New York City, U.S.A.

My grandparents had to pick up their passports and have them documented by a sub-prefect in Acireale, a coastal town on Sicily's eastern coast which functioned as a county seat in military and civic transactions at that time. Acireale is north of the city of Catania and 40 miles from Randazzo, approximately a two-hour car drive today, but probably a two-day mule ride in 1920.

From the date of their marriage, Francesco Paolo and Antonia had five months to prepare for departure and the separation from their families and fellow villagers that would follow—this at a time when they were just becoming acquainted with one another.

The newlyweds left Randazzo with another couple, Giuseppe and Domenica Caggige and their two sons, Vincenzo and Raymond. Since Domenica was pregnant with her third child, Antonia offered to care for the younger child, Raymond, during the crossing.

The Scafidis and Caggiges traveled west across the island to Palermo, in what was Antonia's first glimpse of her motherland beyond the villages of Castiglione di Sicilia and Randazzo.

On August 30, 1920, Francesco Paolo and Antonia purchased their visas from the American Consulate Service in Palermo, at a cost of 20 lire/$1.00 for Francesco's and 40 lire/$2.00 for Antonia's, with an additional lire/$.05 each for authentication by a prefect.

The next day, August 31, 1920, they boarded their ship and left Sicily behind.

*Left: First page of Francesco's passport (top) and stamped page from Antonia's passport (bottom). Above: Antonia's passenger ticket for the immigrant ship, Columbia.*

*"The Columbia," from the Andreas Hernandez Collection, courtesy of The Statue of Liberty–Ellis Island Foundation, Inc.*

## CHAPTER IV
## THE CROSSING

| | |
|---|---|
| *Congedio* | LEAVE-TAKING |
| *Fior tricolore,* | TRI-COLORED FLOWER, |
| *tramontano le stelle* | STARS GO DOWN |
| *in mezzo al mare* | FAR OUT AT SEA |
| *e si spengono I canti entro il mio core.* | AND IN MY HEART SONGS DIE. |

*Giosue Carducci (1835-1907)*

The Scafidis and Caggiges were counted among the 1,303 immigrant passengers who left Palermo, Sicily aboard the Columbia, a 503' long British flag ship from the Triestina Navigation Line that crept across the Atlantic at 17.3 miles an hour (15 knots). They traveled third class or "steerage," the least expensive accommodations in the lowest reaches of the ship.

A typical steamship's steerage section, the large compartment in its bottom deck where steering mechanisms are located, could accommodate over 1,000 passengers. These quarters were crowded, often unsanitary, and the breeding grounds for contagious diseases. Hair lice were common. Prior to disembarking, female passengers were often deloused to kill lice; the less fortunate were subjected to unceremonious haircuts upon arrival at Ellis Island.

Sleeping quarters in steerage consisted of narrow bunk beds, packed two to three high, in long rows. The air was rank, heavy with smoke and the odors of seasickness and bodies pressed together without adequate amenities for basic hygiene. Depending on the ship, food was served at long tables, or doled out in compartmented lunch buckets with lids to be eaten on bunk beds.

During the rough Atlantic crossing, many of the third class passengers experienced seasickness and remained in their bunks. I can imagine the toll the trip took on Antonia, in the first trimester of her first pregnancy, and on her pregnant friend, Domenica. The crossing was to take sixteen days; they were aboard the ship for nineteen.

Those who were not seasick left steerage for the upper decks where they stayed outside singing, playing instruments, and dancing. Since some of the emigrating passengers, like my grandfather, had made the trip before, there was lots of talk about what would happen on Ellis Island. The anxiety levels of the uninitiated must have mounted as they crossed off the days.

The Scafidis' passenger tickets for the Columbia noted that they were each entitled to one bed and a space not to exceed one-half cubic meter. They were allowed 100 kg of luggage, approximately 220 pounds, per person.

When my sister and I were young girls, sharing a bedroom with a walk-in closet, my grandmother gave each of us one of the steamer trunks that carried all of her personal and household possessions across the Atlantic. The *casse* had been filled with her *corredo sposa trousseau*—linens and house furnishings that Sicilian brides were expected to bring to their marriage, just as the groom was expected to provide his wife with gold jewelry and a house.

Nearly 70 years after the crossing, when I was engaged to be married, Nana passed along parts of her trousseau to me—the ensemble of wedding jewelry given to her by my grandfather and a handmade nightdress, which may have been worn on her wedding night, since it has an intricately crocheted white bodice attached to a long muslin skirt.

Francesco Paolo and Antonia were among the fortunate to have possessions to bring with them. Some immigrants traveled with only the clothes on their backs, while others carried an empty piece of luggage to cover up the embarrassment of their poverty.

When the Columbia navigated through New York's Harbor, the passengers were greeted by the colossal symbol of freedom and democracy—*Lady Liberty*—reaching 305 feet into the sky. The Columbia's passengers, as well as the emigrant millions who proceeded and followed them past the Statue of Liberty, would have been comforted to know the words of a sonnet, *The New Colossus*, inscribed in its base.

*Not like the brazen giant of Greek fame*
*With conquering limbs astride from land to land;*
*Here at our sea-washed, sunset gates shall stand*
*A mighty woman with a torch, whose flame*
*Is the imprisoned lightning, and her name*
*Mother of Exiles. From her beacon-hand*
*Glows world-wide welcome; her mild eyes command*
*The air-bridged harbor that twin cities frame,*
*"Keep, ancient lands, your storied pomp!" cries she*
*With silent lips. "Give me your tired, your poor,*
*Your huddled masses yearning to breathe free,*
*The wretched refuse of your teeming shore,*
*Send these, the homeless, tempest-tossed to me,*
*I lift my lamp beside the golden door."*

—Emma Lazarus, New York City, 1883

Just beyond the Statue of Liberty, one mile from the tip of Manhattan, the sprawling Ellis Island came into view. From 1892 until 1954 when it was closed, this bustling oasis in New York's harbor, served as the primary immigration center for the United States—the "front doors to freedom" for over 20 million immigrants.

Rather than stop at Ellis Island, the steamships inched slowly toward the next island and the immense city of Manhattan. Most of the new arrivals in third class had never seen houses with electricity, no less the blazing lights of skyscrapers against the Manhattan and Brooklyn skylines.

Their steamships docked in New York City's Hudson or East River piers, where first- and second-class passengers underwent a cursory inspection aboard the steamship before walking off the ship and passing through customs in Manhattan. These more affluent passengers, who could afford higher-priced tickets, were considered less likely to become public liabilities.

The third class passengers, however, were jammed into barges run by the U.S. Immigration Service and transported from the Manhattan pier back to Ellis Island, where everyone was required to undergo a medical and legal inspection. During the busy spring to fall shipping season, as many as 10,000–15,000 new arrivals had to wait aboard their ships for days without adequate food, water or facilities before being ferried to Ellis Island. This probably accounts for the three extra days, beyond the 16 anticipated for the crossing, that the Columbia's passengers from Palermo were on board their ship. The delay, with their destination so close and their hopes so high, must have been agonizing.

If that was indeed the case, it was a weary group of 740 third class passengers who finally reached Ellis Island on September 18, 1920. They were among 3,000–6,000 immigrants processed at the island's center on each average 12-hour workday. If an immigrant's papers were in order and his health reasonably good, the inspection took four to six hours.

Beginning in 1893, the United States required steamer companies to record vital statistics for each passenger by asking them 33 questions at the point of debarkation. Their answers were recorded on long lines across the ship manifest, approximately 30 passengers to a page. Each line was assigned a sequential number, which was used to identify the passenger throughout the inspection process. So it was that Francesco had a number "7" paper tag pinned to his jacket, and Antonia a number "14," as they made their way down the barge's gang plank to set foot on their newly adopted country.

*The Manhattan skyline as seen through a window in the Great Hall of the Registry Room on Ellis Island, April 2008.*

## CHAPTER V
## ELLIS ISLAND THEN

*Chistu munnu e fattu a scala; cu lu scinnie e cu l'acchiana.*
THE WORLD IS LIKE A STAIRCASE; SOME GO UP AND SOME GO DOWN.

The lines of arriving immigrants wound from the island's docks to the first floor *Baggage Room*, where they could leave their luggage before proceeding up the long open stairway to the *Registry Room*. Surely Antonia glanced over her shoulder more than once, after leaving her life's possessions behind in an anonymous pile of bundles, baskets, burlap bags, suitcases, and trunks.

The screening process began immediately with Medical Inspectors—physicians dressed in uniforms at the top the stairs—peering down the line of immigrants as they ascended. Those showing visible signs of questionable health were immediately pulled from the line for further examination.

The legal and medical inspections took place in the *Great Hall* of the *Registry Room*, a grand space with vaulted, tiled ceilings, balconies, and American flags that must have overwhelmed those coming from the tight quarters of steerage. The views of New York City's awesome skylines framed in the windows resembled the fairyland images from Antonia's childhood folk tales beyond the abilities of her own imagination.

The new arrivals were semi-organized into a maze of lines that funneled into penned-in areas. The hot, crowded room echoed with a cacophony of nearly deafening sound. Ellis Island records indicate that as many as 50 different languages were spoken at the same time in this 20th-century

*Tower of Babel.* Antonia and others were hearing languages other than their own, for the first time.

The medical inspectors did not have long to diagnose a list of 60 illnesses. They first checked for lice and measles, which were common. Children, especially, succumbed to the contagious illnesses that bred in steerage. Everyone was examined for trachoma, a highly contagious eye infection that can lead to blindness. While the condition was virtually unheard of in the United States, it was common in Eastern Europe. The eyes were scrutinized by raising the eyelids with a finger, hairpin, or, most commonly, a buttonhook! If a child was found to have trachoma, he had to return to his homeland with a parent, regardless if there was no home left.

Those determined physically or mentally deficient were given a chalk mark on their clothing and detained. For instance, a chalked "E" referred to a condition of the eye, "H" referred to the heart, and "S" meant mentally unstable or insane.

Pregnant women were not allowed to enter the country. Luckily, Antonia slipped by without any visible signs of her three-month pregnancy. Otherwise, she would have been detained on Ellis Island until the birth of her child in the hospital maternity ward, where over 350 babies were born during the immigration center's years of operation.

With a medical staff of 40 physicians, the U.S. Public Service operated Ellis Island's 15 building medical facility that housed 725 hospital beds. Over 3,500, including more than 1,400 children, died on Ellis Island, cementing its dual reputation as the *Island of Tears* as well as the *Island of Hope*.

For the majority of immigrants who passed medical inspection, all lines led to the immigration inspectors standing behind tall desks piled high with hand-written, difficult-to-decipher ship manifests. The inspectors' primary task was to cross-examine new arrivals and verify their answers to the 33 questions they had been asked at the start of their journey. The immigration officers, who could barely understand the immigrants, relied on translators for answers to their rapid-fire questions in a two-minute examination.

Fortunately for Antonia, and so many other illiterate immigrants, the translators were generally softhearted. Rather than participate in the alien's deportation, they would interpret to the immigrant's benefit.

> *These men of many nations must be taught American ways,*
> *the English language, and the right way to live.*
> —Henry Ford, on immigrants

Starting in 1917, as a result of swelling anti-immigration forces in the U.S., all immigrants 16 years and older had to read a 40-word passage in their native language to gain entry. If the inspectors suspected illiteracy, the immigrant was asked to draw three diamonds to see if they were used to holding a pencil. The only mark unschooled Antonia could make was an "X." The Columbia's third class passengers may have arrived on too busy a day for the administration of literacy tests, or it may have been that wives of literate men were not tested.

It was also required that all immigrants enter the country with a minimum of $20.00, a requirement that gave rise to the illegal industry of momentarily loaning new arrivals $20.00 in bills for the princely rental sum of $2.00. At the time of their departure from Palermo, most of those recorded on the ship manifest page with my grandfather declared $15.00 to $50.00 in cash assets. Upon arrival at Ellis Island, Francesco's beginning bankroll of $15.00 bulged to $80.00, as noted by the inspector. Having made a previous trip to the United States, Francesco may have thought it unwise to declare his financial worth at the start of the trip, or he may have rented $65.00, which seems less likely, given the additional expenses he still had to face.

Intentionally or not, and certainly not by official order, several immigrants received new names at the inspection desk. The foreign sounding names were simplified, changed, and "Americanized" by the inspectors. Somewhere along the way, Franceso Paolo became Frank and Antonia was changed to the similarly spelled name of French origin, Antoinette.

Despite the rigors of inspection, eighty percent of the immigrants who arrived on Ellis Island were passed through. One-third of them stayed in New York City. A suspicious 10% were held on the island for a legal hearing to determine if they were "liable to become a public charge." Of the twenty percent who were detained for a legal hearing, medical reasons, or for lack of funds for transportation off the island, only two percent were sent back to their homelands, sometimes dividing families.

Behind the row of inspectors' desks were the *Stairs of Separation*, leading in three different directions. The detained were led down the middle stairway to an extended limbo. Those with family or friends eager to meet them, took the left staircase, leading to a waiting room. Upon entering, their names were called out, usually triggering an emotional reunion. Women, who were not allowed to leave Ellis Island unaccompanied, often married on the spot, paying a steep admission price for the privilege of entering the new world.

Francesco Paolo and Antonia left the *Registration Room* via the stairs on the right, entering an area where they could exchange currency, purchase railroad tickets for their final destination, and buy their first "American food"—a box lunch consisting of a sandwich, piece of fruit, and a slice of pie priced at 50 cents to a dollar.

Con men also awaited some unfortunate new arrivals at the money exchange and railroad ticket counters, where immigrant dollars were exchanged for pennies and train fares were pocketed, sending immigrants on wild goose chase rides as their first experience in the United States.

Despite the ship manifest notation that the Scafidi couple was bound for "Roodland, New York," we presume that they successfully purchased train tickets for Rutland, Vermont and continued their journey, weary but somewhat relieved at having made it thus far. This time, Francesco Paolo and Antonia were pinned with a new paper tag giving the name of their final destination and assigning their fate to a railroad conductor.

I find it particularly poignant that my grandparents, along with all the other immigrants listed on the same page of the Columbia's ship manifest, answered the 20th question, "Length of time alien intends to reside in the United States?" with "ALWAYS."

*The Battery at the foot of Manhattan Island, April 2008.*

## CHAPTER VI
## ELLIS ISLAND TODAY

*Pianu pianu se va luntanu.*
LITTLE BY LITTLE ONE GOES VERY FAR.

Over 100 million Americans trace their ancestry to the immigrants who passed through Ellis Island before dispersing across the country. In late April 2008, I had a small taste of their experience in a reverse migration from Vermont to Ellis Island.

On a cool spring day, I arrived at Battery Park in lower Manhattan, just blocks from the infamous September 11, 2001 World Trade Center destruction site then under reconstruction. For what seemed like an interminable four hours, I stood in a long line of multi-nationals that wrapped around the ticket office in Castle Clinton, waiting to board a ferry to Ellis Island.

The wait was not without pleasant diversion. Pink and white cherry blossoms wafted to the ground with the slightest whisper of wind. Nonchalant gray squirrels posed like bored celebrities for tourists behind digital cameras. Bored tourists nibbled Coney Island hot dogs and soft pretzels topped with deli mustard in mid-morning. The cacophony of city sounds—cabs, delivery trucks, vendors, buskers, bikers, and joggers—mingled with the conversational chatter in French, Italian, Indian, Spanish, German, Ukranian, Pakistani, Russian, Chinese.... Further up the line, a merry pack of Italians requested "Santa Lucia" from the Jamaican kettle drummer, who happily obliged to the delight of everyone within hearing distance.

In our post-9/11 world, the park was surrounded by the NYPD with revved-up German Shepherd police dogs tugging on leashes. Before boarding the ferry, I was required to pass through security lines and detection equipment, removing outer clothing, belt, hat, and shoes, while tossing camera, knapsack, watch, jewelry, and pocket change into bins on conveyor belts. On the other side of the invasive screening devices, I redressed among strangers and moved into a staging area where we were penned together, flesh to flesh, with the echo of 50 different languages and a growing sense of crowd unrest. Finally, a ferry docked and I was pushed to the gangplank, past the sniffing police dogs, caught up in a race for a seat and the welcome relief of being off my feet.

A real Vermonter rushes to freedom in the open-air top deck, regardless of the wind and threatening rain. I had my reward in the breathtaking views of the Manhattan skyline as best appreciated from the open harbor. My close encounter with the majestic Lady Liberty and the exciting approach to Ellis Island, in its spring splendor, seemed extremely welcoming.

Despite the rigors of my grandparents' trip, I believe that Ellis Island seemed, and indeed was, equally welcoming to them in the dog days of their late summer arrival, 88 years earlier. Unlike immigrants from other parts of Eastern Europe, they were not being driven from their homeland by a dominant or an oppressive force. They could have stayed in Sicily and survived, but they might not have prospered. They needed America as a refuge from their island's dead end deprivation and America needed them to help fuel its post WWI industrial economy. Immigration officers, translators, medical inspectors, moneychangers, and railroad conductors wanted to, and did, help them along the way.

When I first visited Ellis Island in 1996, a few years after its renovation and re-opening as a national historic landmark, I was swept up in the drama and the overwhelming sense of separation, loss, sacrifice, and negative stereotypes that seemed to characterize the immigrant experience. I was unable to balance the conflicting forces of courage and rejection. The positive aspects of my grandparents' emigration were not visible to me. Instead, I remembered the "Poor Papa and Mama" stories of my childhood.

On this return trip, I was better able to intellectually engage with the immigrant experience and to revel in my grandparents' participation which, by then, I had spent several years researching. This time I could

*Ellis Island, April 2008.*

*The author at the Wall of Immigrants, July 4, 1996.*

*Ellis Island Today*

toast their bravery and share their sense of adventure and excitement. I was excited to flesh out more of the details and I looked forward to once again running my fingers across the name of Antonia D. Scafidi etched on the Wall of Immigrants that stretches around the island's outer seawall overlooking New York harbor.

The opportunity to add immigrants' names to the monument wall was part of a creative fund-raising effort that started in 1984 to restore Ellis Island. President Ronald Reagan appointed Lee Iacocca, automobile industry executive and son of Italian immigrants, to head the Statue of Liberty-Ellis Island Foundation. The $160 million dollar project was the largest historic restoration in U.S. history, and I wanted my timid, little grandmother to be part of it—to stand alone and be individually recognized, outside of the great American melting pot, in the lasting promise of stone. And, there you will find her, on panel #387, second column from the left, the 24th name down from the top.

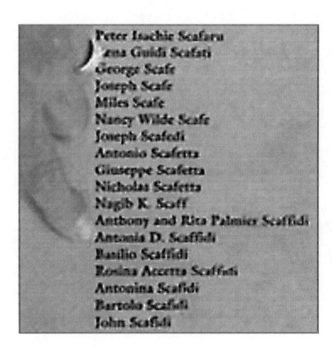

41

*Merchant's Row, Rutland, Vermont in the 1920s with trolley tracks visible in the foreground. The trolley lines, which were in operation when my grandparents arrived, stopped service in 1923. Courtesy of the Rutland Historical Society.*

## CHAPTER VII
## RANDAZZO TO RUTLAND

*Cu s'aiuta, Diu l'aiuta.*
GOD HELPS THOSE WHO HELP THEMSELVES.

The ship's manifest records that the Scafidi couple was scheduled to join Francesco's older brother Salvatore in Rutland. Upon arrival they were welcomed by the Forest Street family of Giuseppe Foti, one of the first citizens of Randazzo to arrive in Rutland fourteen years earlier (July 1906). My grandparents and the Caggige family stayed with the Fotis until they found places to live in the neighborhood.

It is not known exactly when and why Rutland was originally chosen to become "Little Randazzo." However, once started, the community of like souls in the southwestern section of the city satisfied the Sicilian sense of localism imported with their mistrust of others—often defined as "anyone who did not live within hearing distance of the local church bell." (The Sicilian tendency to be guarded with outsiders is understandable given the island's distressing heritage of repeated invasion, conquest, and foreign domination. Equally intense is the overwhelming hospitality and loyalty that replace distrust when friendship is established.)

Most Italians who came to the United States during the peak years of emigration sought *paesani*, groups of immigrants from the same village or *paese*. Amidst the perplexing cauldron of social and cultural differences, the village ties endured in tight neighborhoods that provided the comforts of familiar dialects, food, and friends sharing a similar experience. Once settled into homes and jobs, Randazzo transplants sent word back to family and friends in Sicily, paving the way for others to follow.

In "A History of St. Peter's Parish, Rutland, Vermont," author Patrick T. Hannon notes that the number of Italians in the Rutland area grew from seven families in 1893 to approximately 800 in 1907. The community bulged, reaching its peak in the late 1920s and early 1930s.

"Why Rutland?" may be an easier question to answer. When my grandparents arrived in 1920, the city was the third largest in the state with a population of 14,954. From 1910 to 1930, Rutland experienced the largest growth spurts of its history with population increases averaging fifteen percent for each of the three decades. The city's impressive expansion is rooted in its prized marble quarries and the railroads built to support the burgeoning industry.

In the early 1800s, small, high-quality deposits of marble were discovered in Rutland and, in the 1830s, a massive deposit of nearly solid white marble was found in what is now West Rutland. Within a decade, small companies had begun quarrying operations, employing English and Irish immigrants already in the area. The Rutland region quickly became one of the leading producers of marble in the world.

In 1880, when Colonel Redfield Proctor, a former Vermont governor and U.S. Senator, established the Vermont Marble Company, its expansion was hampered by the limited availability of skilled stonecutters and sculptors. Colonel Proctor recruited marble craftsmen from what was then the world center of the marble industry, Carrara in Tuscany, Italy. Although the Italian marble was prized, the famous quarries were considered nearly unworkable because of their extreme depth. The Colonel successfully convinced five skilled craftsmen from Carrara to practice their art and to teach apprentices at the Vermont Marble Company. Arriving in 1882, these pioneers are believed to be the first Italian immigrants to settle in the Rutland region.

There soon followed a second wave of Italian marble workers from Carrara along with a steady procession of northern Italians from other professions—tailors, barbers, store owners, and importers to provide the staples the marble workers were accustomed to in their homeland. Given the similar topography and climate of northern Italy, immigrants from that region did not find it difficult to adjust to central Vermont, particularly when they began to establish communities.

As word spread back across the Atlantic, a third wave of immigrants, this time from the warmer climates of southern Italy and Sicily, arrived in

*World War I era photo of Louis Cereghino's New York Fruit Market on 38 Center Street in Rutland. The five figures in the foreground are (left to right): Mrs. Rachel Cereghino, employee Mollie Mahoney, Rose Dolphino Theresa (young girl in front of Ms. Mahoney), Louis Cereghino, and Mary Cereghino (Lanzillo). The three background figures are customer friends.*
*Courtesy of the Rutland Historical Society.*

*The Garafano (Carnation) Italian Ice Stand on Rutland's West Street. An Orange Crush advertising sign is visible on the front. The stand was located on the north side of West Street across from Marro's Store. The Garafano house (not visible) was to the left of the stand. The occupants of the car are unidentified. Courtesy of the Rutland Historical Society.*

*In 1929 Rutland built a municipal swimming pool on the western side of North Main Street. This municipal facility became not only a notable public recreation site but also a popular postcard view. Courtesy of the Rutland Historical Society.*

Rutland. (The more typical emigration pattern favored larger cities and railroad centers.) Unskilled in the marble industry and generally more passive in nature, they found work with the railroad companies or foundries that were integral to Rutland's reputation as a blue-collar town. They did manual labor, averaging 10-hour days for a prevailing wage of $1.25 per day. Others quickly started businesses needed by the community, using their talents or relying on training they had received in Italy.

In sharp contrast to the stagnating conditions in Sicily, Rutland offered a smorgasbord of opportunities to its new citizens in 1920. Relieved of the uncertainties of wartime, the United States was also flexing its prosperity muscle at the dawn of the "Roaring Twenties"—the "Jazz Age," a decade that would crash in the Great Depression.

It was a Presidential election year when my grandparents arrived in September. Warren G. Harding and James M. Cox were vying for the highest office in the land at the tail end of President Woodrow Wilson's term.

The 19th Amendment to the U.S. Constitution had passed just days before the Columbia docked in New Your Harbor, guaranteeing women the right to vote in the upcoming election and for the first time in the country's history. Imagine—the promise of being heard to those like my grandmother who barely had a voice in their homelands. For her, and for so many others, it would take another generation to break the patterns of deeply ingrained silence and cultural inhibitions.

Commercial radio's development, put on hold during World War I, was jump-started by the Presidential elections. In November, the first broadcasting license was issued and, a short time later, retail stores were advertising parlor "companion" radios for $10.00, featuring wood finishes and cathedral styling.

The average income in 1920 was $2,160; the average cost of a new house was $6,296 and a new car could be purchased for $525. A gallon of gas was 13 cents, a loaf of bread 12 cents, and a gallon of milk 67 cents.

Al Jolson and soprano Lucy Gates were popular Columbia recording artists, while the one-step and the foxtrot were the rage on the dance floor. *Look for the Silver Lining*, *When My Baby Smiles at Me*, and *I'll Be*

*With You in Apple Blossom Time* were top hits of the year. Charlie Chaplin was a major box office attraction in *The Kid*.

The Boston Red Sox, considered the best baseball team in the country, traded the larger than life Babe Ruth to the New York Yankees for $125,000, the largest sum ever paid for a player until that time. Just the year before, on October 1st, the young home run king traveled to Rutland, Vermont with his Red Sox teammates to play the local Rutland Royals. Nothing like that had ever happened before.

On January 16th, Prohibition began with the passage of the 18th Amendment to the U.S. Constitution. The legislation spawned a bootleg industry that would last for the next thirteen years but only serve to spark the collective creativity of Rutland's wine-loving Sicilians.

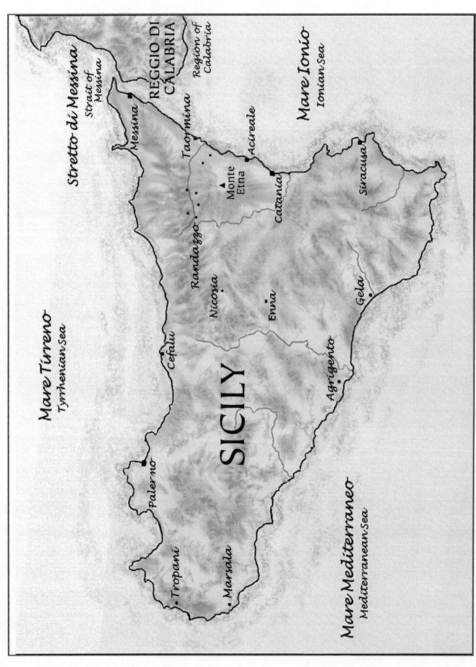

The triangular island of Sicily is the largest (9,925 square miles) in the Mediterranean. It is divided into nine provinces, running clockwise around the coast: Palermo, Messina, Catania, Syracuse, Caltanissetta, Agrigento, Trapani, and landlocked Enna in the middle.

## CHAPTER VIII
## RETURN TO RANDAZZO

*Senza famiglia, non sei niete.*
WITHOUT FAMILY, YOU ARE NOTHING.

I arrived in Randazzo on a rainy day in October 2007 with skies as gray and black as the lava rock used to build the ancient city. Looming large, just as it had for my grandparents, is the capricious Mt. Etna, Sicily's most prominent landmark and one of the world's most active volcanoes. Reaching over two miles into the sky, Etna is breathtakingly beautiful in its domination of the region. Sicilians, who live with its unpredictability, refer to Etna simply as "The Mountain," or *Mongibello* (*Muncibeddu*, in dialect).

Randazzo lies at the volcano's northern base, surrounded by lava fields, on the banks of the Alcantara River. While the origin of the city's name is not certain, it is thought to derive from Randaches, the name of a Byzantine governor of Taormina, a coastal town on the Ionian Sea, also in the province of Catania. Today, Randazzo refers to itself as the "Guardian of the Mountain"—quite a name to live up to when the mountain is Etna and averages one eruption every six years.

The lower slopes of Mt. Etna around Randazzo are extremely fertile, with large tracts of land cultivated with olives, prickly pears, lemons, oranges, tangerines, and other citrus fruits brought to Sicily by its various conquerors. Some of these crops at the mountain's base produce five harvests a year, which is why Sicilian farmers return to Etna's rich, black soil after each volcanic eruption.

Farther up the mountainside are plantations of pistachios, walnuts, almonds, and chestnuts. The prized Etna mushroom is heavily foraged and sold in Randazzo's piazza markets as the star ingredient for antipasto,

soups, pastas, risotto, pizza, and a variety of local meat dishes. The mushroom's unique perfume and taste derive from the pine, chestnut, and birch trees in Etna's mountainside forests, as well as from a variety of fragrant wild herbs in the undergrowth. Vineyards ring the lava fields around Randazzo, becoming denser on the city's eastern outskirts and beyond. The traditions of the region's agro-economy have remained unchanged for centuries.

While it is a medieval city, Randazzo shares the island's history of early settlement, as far back as 12,000 BC, followed by centuries of conquest by the Carthaginians from North Africa, the Greeks, Romans, Byzantines, Arabs, the Lombards from Northern Italy, the Normans, Spanish, and British. What remains of its medieval architectural magnificence are crumbled portions of a once stately castle and the three kilometers of lava rock wall with eight guard towers that surround the old city.

Randazzo is situated in the foothills of Sicily's mountainous interior, a region that affords a more traditional Sicilian life than any other area of the island. The harsh and dramatic landscape has sentenced centuries of inhabitants to powerful isolation. Time-warped towns trickle down steep mountainsides—vestiges of the island's feudal period when aristocratic landlords forced peasants to resettle in these close living quarters. In the distance, between silhouetted Norman castles, forts, landmark *duomos*, and large multi-storey stone houses, are fields of wheat, the mainstay of Sicilian agriculture for 2,000 years. The vast, undulating landscape is occasionally interrupted by miniature orchards.

Randazzo's settlers chose proximity to the Alcantara River at the base of Mt. Etna rather than a mountain stronghold to establish a community. In 1536, when Randazzo, Messina, and Palermo reigned as Sicily's three largest cities, a lava flow destroyed much of Randazzo, sending it into a prolonged decline from which it never fully recovered.

*Mt. Etna as seen from the city of Randazzo, October 2007.*

*The beautiful hilltop town of Gangi,
en route from Nicosia to Randazzo, October 2007.*

*On the approach to Randazzo, miles of freshly plowed wheat fields ready for planting, October 2007.*

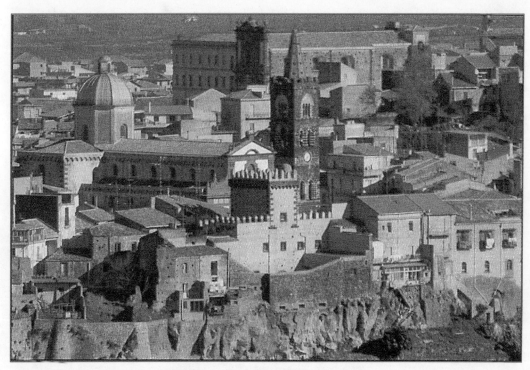

*Randazzo, Sicily (population 11,700).*

During the next 300 years, economic conditions in Randazzo, not unlike the rest of Sicily, deteriorated to the point that the island became the world's main source of emigration by 1900.

The Industrial Revolution barely brushed Sicily, Italy's largest region. Jobs were scarce and doled out through a corrupt, lingering system of feudalism and nepotism. Meager wages, amounting to a few cents for twelve or more hours of work a day, were no match for the high cost of living and taxation. In the face of over-population and mass poverty, food could not be stretched far enough. Sicilians fled to Catania and Palermo, the island's largest cities, or north to the Italian mainland in search of work. To relieve the increasingly dire situation, the Italian government issued special passports to promote emigration to other countries.

Married just one month, Francesco Paulo and Antonia DelPopolo Scafidi applied for two of those special passports to the United States of America in April 1920. They were part of the mass exodus of two million Sicilians who emigrated to the U.S. between 1890 and 1920. They were among the lucky ones.

In 1943, during World War II, American Allies dropped bombs on the two bridges crossing the Alcantara River to prevent the occupying German army from proceeding across Sicily to Messina and, from there, to the Italian mainland. The bombing destroyed eighty percent of Randazzo, nearly obliterating its architectural heritage, while killing and/or displacing 6,000 of the city's residents.

Nearly six decades later, the city remains cloaked in the somber evidence of war. It is a study in missing parts and pieces—crumbling arches, gaping mortar holes, liberated lava rock, chained doors—creating an overwhelming sense of abandonment.

Rebuilding within the "old city" and the "new city" that rings it has been haphazard and set back by yet another lava flow in 1981. Unlike Pompeii, Randazzo has not been mummified by volcanic dust. It continues to live in Etna's shadow. Despite its missing parts, pieces, and people, the family ties that bind generations, over a century and across the Atlantic Ocean to those who remember, remain unbroken.

*St. Maria's Basillica on Randazzo's Basillica Square, October 2007.*

## CHAPTER IX
## FINDING FRANCESCO PAOLO

*Curri quannu vo,' che ca t'aspettu.*
RUN WHENEVER YOU WILL, FOR I SHALL AWAIT YOU HERE.

For centuries, Randazzo's crown jewels have been its three churches situated on the piazzas, the municipal squares that bear their names.

St. Maria's Basillica, *la Chiesa di S. Maria,* on Basillica Square, was completely constructed of lava stone starting in the thirteenth century. In the 19th century when my grandfather lived in Randazzo, the church was called a cathedral and Cathedral Square, which surrounded it, was the neighborhood's gathering place. One of the streets radiating from its center, *Strada Commissione*, is a long, narrow cobblestone passage lined with small, two-storey, lava stone row houses with thick wooden doors and clay tile roofs.

*No. 10.92 Strada Commissione* was home to Vincenzo (born September 13, 1849, died December 10, 1935) and Venera Arcey Scafidi (born July 27, 1853, died December 30, 1927) and their nine children:

    Antonio (born June 28, 1875)
    Lorenzo (born August 26, 1877)
    Salvatore (born September 21, 1878)
    Maria (born December 6, 1882, died February 28, 1887)
    Salvatore (born December 16, 1884, died July 4, 1972)
    Giuseppa (born May 26, 1887, died December 28, 1887)
    Francesco Paolo (born November 20, 1888, died December 2, 1958)
    Mariano (born January 7, 1891)
    Rosario (born November 30, 1896)

*#10 Via De Quatris, formerly called No. 10.92 Strada Commissione, home of Vincenzo and Venera Scafidi and birthplace of their son, Francesco Paolo Scafidi, October 2007.*

*Behind a decorative wrought iron fence, #12 and #14 Via De Quatris share a stone courtyard with the Scafidi house. The houses' lava rock walls are riddled with mortar shell holes from World War II bombing raids, October 2007.*

Since the children were born over a 21-year period, they probably did not (I hope) all live in the house at the same time.

After the destruction of World War II, when the streets of Randazzo were renamed and renumbered, Strada Commissione No. 10.92 became Via de Quatris No. 10, which is where I found Vincenzo's and Venera's abandoned house in October 2007. The narrow, two-storey building is set back from the street behind a wrought iron gate, faced by a small courtyard and flanked by two other town houses. While it was difficult to determine how long No. 10 Via de Quatris has been unoccupied, a sapling was growing from its threshold when I visited.

In the long, black ledgers stored in Randazzo's municipal office, there are recorded dates for the death of the two daughters born to Vincenzo and Venera. Giuseppa died at seven months and Maria lived to be 29 years old. Local officials felt that a first-born Salvatore died in his youth and that a second son was named Salvatore in his honor, as was the custom of the time.

Francesco Paolo, child number seven in the Vincenzo and Venera Scafidi household, is the only child in his family with a recorded middle name. I was told that in Sicily he would have commonly been called Ciccu Paulu, the familiar name spoken only by the fellow Sicilians of his inner circle in Rutland. Outside of that community, Francesco was Anglicized to Francis and Frank.

His father, Vincenzo was 86 years old at the time of his death, outliving his younger wife, Venera, by 12 years. Venera, who bore nine children when she was between the ages of 21 to 43, lived to be 71 years old. The surname "Arcey" is of Spanish origin—not a surprising discovery given the centuries of Spain's occupation of Sicily, but certainly new information to me and the other descendants of Venera and Vincenzo. Officials in Randazzo speculated that given my great grandmother's

Italian first name, "Venera," her mother was probably of Italian origin and her father Spanish.

I learned that the original and correct spelling of "Scafidi," as noted in the municipal register and underscored by the city magistrate, is with one "f," although the double-f version, "Scaffidi," appears on most of my grandparent's official documents. No surprise, as the Ellis Island Ship Passenger Records include no fewer than 28 possible spellings of the family name: Scaffidi, Scaffiddi, Scaffiti, Scafidi, Sccaffidi, Scafiddi, Scafiti, Scoffidi, Scofidi, Scaffadi, Scaffedi, Scaffide, Scaffido, Scalfidi, Scavitti, Schafidi, Scheffidi, Scofiti, Scuffidi, Scafedi, Scaffati, Scaffito, Scafida, Scafide, Scafido, Scafodi, Scatidi, and Scifidi!

The Sicilians take a no-nonsense approach to limited cemetery space by excavating older graves and combining the remains in a common site— to the end and beyond they are a social and thrifty lot. I was, however,

able to locate the gravesites of my grandfather's brother Salvatore and his wife Alfia in the Randazzo community cemetery. The Cemetery Commissioner, Arturo Alfonso, whose aunt was a Scafidi, was able to direct me to the house in Montelaguarida where Salvatore and Alfia lived until they died.

In 1958, when Salvatore received word that his younger brother Francesco Paolo had passed away in Vermont, he sent a black-bordered letter of grief and resignation to my grandmother.

The Italian scholar who translated Salvatore's letter, as well as those from other Scafidi and Delpopolo family members, noted that the translations seem stilted because the original Italian is stilted. The writers were used to speaking in rapid Sicilian dialects which were rarely written, even among close family members. Those who went to school learned "proper" Italian which they reverted to for writing. Some of the letters had no punctuation and they were left that way in translation.

Tension and pretension about the language abound throughout Italy. The dialects are so different that people in nearby villages often have difficulty understanding one another. The further south you travel in the country, the more dialects depart from formal Italian.

Conversely, if you speak in a dialect that is recognized in its place of origin, as I did in Randazzo, be prepared to gain instant acceptance and admiration. To my surprise and pleasure, the remembered short phrases and discreet words that I cobbled together into sentences were understood as Randazzesi, the local dialect of my grandfather's hometown.

*Dearest Sister-in-Law*

*Yesterday your letter reached me which talked of the death of my brother. This I had not expected and for me it was a blow to my heart. When we opened the letter and saw the black stripes we did not know before reading it what it might deal with. When I heard of the loss of my brother it was such a blow to my heart and an atrocious pain, all the more in that there is such a distance that we are prevented from all that we should do for all our dear ones to whom the sudden death has caused pain, for when one is ill there is a certain resignation but on this earth we are on a journey and we must resign ourselves to what God does. I would say to my nieces that we are together with you at the death of your father. Antonia I beg you to write me and send me news of you because when there is distance that which gives us comfort is this poor piece of paper.*

*We kiss everyone and take you to our heart, your in-laws*

*Salvatore and Alfia*

Randazzo li 19-12-958

Cognata carissima

Beri mie giunta la vostra lettera, con i quali parlavo della morte di mio fratello, questo non me lo spetavo per me e stato un colpo al cuore, quando abbiamo ~~visto~~ aperto la lettera e abbiamo visto la carta con le striscie neri prima di legerla non si sapeva di chi si tratava, quando o sentito la perdita di

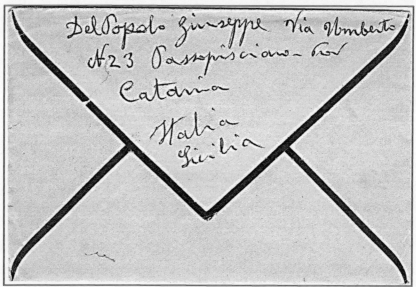

*Finding Francesco Paolo*

There are no members of the Scafidi family alive or traceable through the cemetery ledgers in Randazzo today. Seemingly, the last descendants of Vincenzo and Venera Scafidi to live in the area were Salvatore and Antonio. While the family names are familiar, I do not know to which generation the men belonged. They lived at Numbers 98 and 138 Via Liberta, the main street of Santa Domenica Vittoria, a tiny village about six miles north of Randazzo. I followed the lead there and learned that Salvatore had held the lofty and powerful position of Police Commissioner before relocating to Catania. In this position, Salvatore would have overseen the local *fianza*, Sicily's law enforcement agency that is also responsible for business permits, tax collection, and border control. Antonio's widow, who lives alone at No. 138 Via Liberta, refused to see or to talk to me by telephone.

Eight Scafidis: Antonio, Antonina, Antonnina, Elvira, Guiseppe, Joseta, Muta, and Vincenzo, are listed in Catania's telephone directory.
I suspect that most are second and third generation family members of the Randazzo Scafidi family.

*Ancient olive trees and terraced lava rock walls line the roads around Passopiciaro, October 2007.*

# CHAPTER X
# DISCOVERING ANTONIA'S WORLD

*Chi vo pianu, va sanu e va lutanu.*
WHO GOES SOFTLY, GOES SAFELY AND GOES FAR.

Heading east from Randazzo, the next small village on the northern slopes of Mt. Etna is Passopisciaro. For some unfathomable reason, the name of this land-locked community of sloping vineyards surrounding a tiny, tattered village center translates to "the steps of the fish dealer."

In the absence of fish, Passopisciaro has long-enjoyed a fine reputation for its distinctive "Etna wines" produced mostly from old Nerello Mascalese vines indigenous to this part of Sicily. Local legend has it that Bacchus brought the first plantings and squeezed the first wine from its grapes at the foot of Mt. Etna. While winemaking thrived in the days of Greek and Roman occupation, it was banned entirely by the Arabs who followed. A few brave hearts surreptitiously kept the wine culture alive, preserving the venerable vines and techniques that keep Passopisciaro on the world map.

One of the letters I had translated prior to the October 2007 research trip indicated that my grandmother's only brother, Giuseppe Delpopolo, owned a house in Passopisciaro, on Via Mazoni #5, which I was able to locate and photograph.

Shortly beyond the Passopisciaro village limits, a turn-off from the main road that leads to the eastern coast of Sicily takes you into a lush valley of small-scale vineyards, almond groves, lava stone shelters, cottages, and terraced gardens. This is the *campagna*—a countryside of twists and turns, greenery and wild flowers that contrast so dramatically with the lava fields of gray and black boulders and barren ground that surround Randazzo. As I drove through the canopied roads, one of them suddenly opened to the fairy tale image of a medieval fortress and village perched on a jagged volcanic peak, directly oppo-

site the face of Mt. Etna. The magic of the moment, coupled with the sheer beauty of coral and yellow Castiglione di Sicilia, as seen from this vantage point, was the most memorable sight in a trip already laden with sensational visual images.

The top of Castiglione's rocky spur, over 2,000 feet above sea level, is graced by the ruins of *Castel Leone*, The Leone Castle, a Norman guard post overlooking the Alcantara Valley. However, long before the Normans, the Greeks built an acropolis, the Byzantines a temple, and the Saracens a tower, as evidenced by excavated artifacts from as far back as the 7th century B.C. Archaeologists have further traced Castiglione's deep roots in antiquity to the Early Bronze Age when the hill was already inhabited.

Inside the city walls, I found a village which, except for the tiny cars, trucks, and motorbikes speeding through its tunnel-like streets, has changed very little since the days of Norman and Greek occupation. I wound around narrow stone passages that encircle the main square, Piazza Lauria, to the magistrate's office in the very oldest section of the city, close to the summit.

Given the age of the records I was trying to locate, the language barriers, and the looming afternoon siesta, my search seemed headed for failure

*A lava stone cottage in the midst of an almond orchard on the outskirts of Castiglione di Sicilia, October 2007.*

when one of the officials found the black ledger including Castiglione's first documented census for the period 1870 to 1929 in an old vault. To my delight and near disbelief, I was soon staring at another branch of my great grandparents' family statistics. While I was not allowed to touch the page, the magistrate kindly copied the information, providing historical perspective that bridged language differences with lots of hand gestures and mutual respect for the accomplishment we shared.

I wanted to believe that Nana was thoroughly a country girl, "of the *campagna*"—that she had grown up amongst the wild flowers in one of the small lava rock cottages scattered throughout the valley of vineyards leading up to the walled city. However, the shreds of evidence I found suggest otherwise.

Unlike the Scafidi family records in Randazzo, no street address was given for the Delpopolo residence. I know that Castiglione di Sicilia extends beyond the city walls and that Salvatore Delpopolo's land was located in the countryside. I also know that to reach his vineyard and prepare the noonday meal, Nana had to leave early in the morning and walk some distance up and down hills. The bread was most likely baked in wood-fired field ovens, similar to those I saw in Randazzo's Archeological Museum. Since the vineyards are located on the flat, gently undulating valley floor, the obvious hills are those leading into and out of the walled city, which is also where the evening campfires were held. Reluctantly, I concluded that Nana's family lived in one of the multi-storey houses ringing the city, overlooking the daily whims of Mt. Etna, an experience that she described in fearful terms all the years that she lived among the friendlier Green Mountains of Vermont in the shadow of Killington Peak.

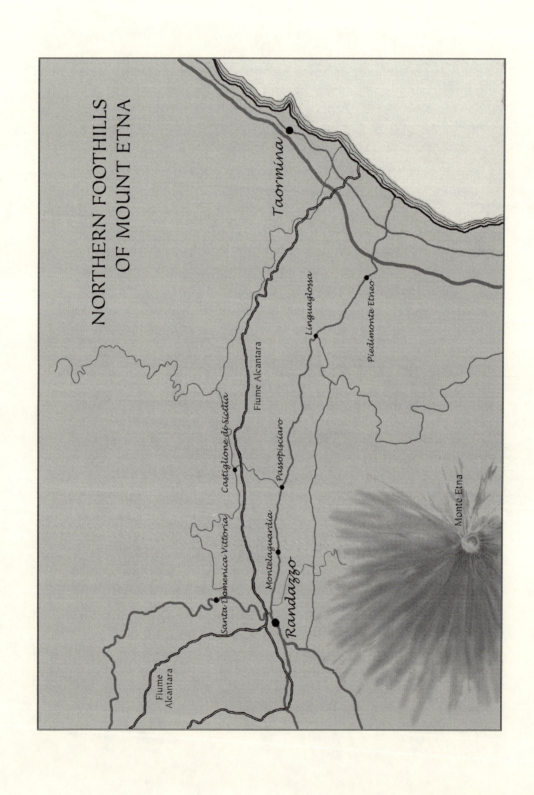

## CHAPTER XI
## THE DELPOPOLOS

*Vo essiri amati di li petri? Prima amari a Diu, poi mamme e patri.*
IF YOU WANT TO BE LOVED BY ALL, FIRST LOVE GOD,
THEN YOUR MOTHER AND FATHER.

Antonia Maria Delpopolo, "Nana," was the first of five children born to Concetta Citra (born April 2, 1870, died September 7, 1939) of Piedmonte Etneo, and Salvatore Delpopolo (born October 23, 1868, died April 25, 1939) of Linguaglossa. Both of Antonia's parents were born in villages further east of Castiglione di Sicilia, in the same region of Catania.

Salvatore and Concetta were married on October 11, 1896. The 1920 census records for Castiglione di Sicilia list Salvatore as "self-employed in the country," which is consistent with the family story that Nana's father owned the vineyard where she met her husband.

The couple's first child, Antonia (born October 18, 1897, died November 20, 1971), was born one year later. She was given the name of her fraternal grandmother, Antonia Spucches, who was married to Leonardo Delpopolo. Salvatore and Concetta followed the Sicilian tradition of honoring the husband's mother by giving their first-born daughter her name.

The rest of Concetta's children were born three years apart, with Giuseppe (born September 2, 1900), the couple's only son, following Antonia, then Maria Concetta (born December 10, 1903) and, finally, twin girls, Giovanna and Antonina (born April 1, 1906).

Nana's brother, Giuseppe, married Sebastiana Zappala (born August 30, 1908); the couple had two children: Concetta (born September 6, 1928), named after Giuseppe's mother, and Salvatore (born November 4, 1934), named after Giuseppe's father.

At the time of their deaths, Giuseppe and his son, Salvatore, were living in the village of Passopisciaro, Giuseppe at Via Regina Margherita #121, which we visited, and Salvatore at Via Manzoni #5, which we were unable to find.

In 1956, Giuseppe's son, Salvatore Delpopolo, sent a letter to my grandparents in Vermont from San Miguel, Buenos Aires, where he was living at the time. He expressed his disappointment at having been misinformed, by the Italian Consulate, about an emigration visa to the United States. He regretfully accepted that he "was destined not to know his dear aunt and uncle (my grandparents) face to face," but would have "to be patient as God wills us to be." He had been told that there was a scarcity of work in the United States and "it seems that those who want to live without working are everywhere, since there's a proverb that says the whole world is a single country, and it's really true that these days the world is half bastardized." At some point, Salvatore returned to Passopisciaro, perhaps to be close to his father, Giuseppe.

In this same letter, Salvatore made reference to his "Aunt Nina and her daughters," who were also living in Buenos Aires at the time. Nina is Antonina, one of Nana's twin sisters. During the years of mass exodus from Sicily, South America, with its familiar Latin culture, became an even more attractive option than the United States to some of the island's citizens on the move. Apparently, it appealed to Nana's twin sisters, since Giovanna also lived in Buenos Aires for some time, as indicated by her correspondence with my grandmother in 1958.

Giovanna married Alfio Pattori. They are listed in the 1920 census as residents of Castiglione di Sicilia, along with their two children: Maria (born September 19, 1927) and Salvatore (born April 21,1933), which suggests that they emigrated to Buenos Aires, as a family, at a later date.

Maria Concetta, Nana's other sister, remained in Sicily all of her life. As a young woman, she relocated to the densely populated Catania, the region's major city, where she raised one son by herself. Maria may have traveled the hardest road of all.

*Antonia Scafidi's younger sister,
Maria Concetta Delpopolo of Catania, Sicily.*

*Young Giovanna Delpopolo,
one of Antonia Scafidi's twin sisters.*

*Maria Concetta Delpopolo with her son.*

In 1971, when she received word of Nana's death, Maria wrote a wrenching letter of condolence to her niece, Concetta Scafidi Miglis, who became the Scafidi family's primary contact with "the other side" after my grandfather died. By then, Maria was 68 years old. She had last seen her older sister when she was 17, fifty-one years before.

> *My Dear Niece,*
>
> *Having received your letter I learned with great sorrow of the loss of your mother, that is my adored sister. I am much grieved to send to all my heartfelt condolences, to all the sisters, in laws and nieces and nephews all. My greatest pain is not to be able to see her. I'll wear mourning so very long for my beloved sister, and I weep so much for my great sorrow. If you have photographs of your mother and father alone send me one. I want only of them because I have them of all the others.*
>
> *I renew my most heartfelt condolences. I kiss all the sisters and families.*
>
> *Your Aunt Delpopolo Maria*

Giuseppe responded to the news of his older sister's passing with a deeply moving letter of sympathy to her daughters. Giuseppe, who was 71 years old at the time, had last seen Antonia when he was 19 years old.

> *Dearest Niece,*
>
> *With great sorrow deep in our heart we received the sad and painful news of the passing of your dear and beloved mother our dear sister and sister-in-law. You cannot imagine the great pain in our heart. It was like such a sudden stab in the heart. The last letter that we received said that she was well and now, imagine, we suddenly hear this sad news so that there is no peace in our heart and, especially since we will not be able to see her again, it gives us yet more pain, but there is nothing more to do since God will give all of us a holy destiny and nothing is left but to pray to God to bring her soul to paradise. My dear nieces I beg you not because there is no longer a papa and mama but because we are desirous to hear from you if you could find someone who can write in Italian so that every once in a while you might write which to us is a joy to get news of you even if we don't know each other but we love you a lot and thus are desirous of news of you. We over here share your great pain to which God makes you resign yourselves. With nothing else to say, we end here. Many fond kisses to your sisters along with their families and to you and your family from us all, hugs and kisses we are your fond uncle and aunt*
>
> *Giueseppe and Sebastiana*

*Giuseppe Delpopolo sent this photograph of himself in his gardens to his older sister, Antonia.*

Giuseppe also sent an emotional, black-bordered condolence letter to his sister, Antonia, in 1958 after receiving word that her husband, Francesco Paolo, had died on December second.

> *Dearest sister and sister-in-law*
>
> *Through our sister Maria I got the sad and painful news of the death of your dear husband, our beloved brother-in-law. All of us associate ourselves with your great pain. For us it was a great sorrow to hear this sad news especially since we are so far away that we cannot see or be present for everything, but there's nothing that can be done about that. Thus in the world we are born in order to die and there is nothing to do but resign one's self to the will of God and nothing is left but to pray to God to bring one's soul to paradise. Dear and Beloved sister and sister-in-law, I can not find words to write to comfort you or give you courage because our eyes are full of tears from this painful news. Only God can comfort you and over time give you a modicum of courage and you should not lose heart because you are in the midst of your dear children and little grandchildren and they will give you a bit of comfort and company. Enough. I cannot prolong my writing so much because our hearts are sad. Once again Have courage and holy resignation and receive kisses from my daughter and we kiss our dear nieces and their families and from us receive a strong embrace and kisses and we are your sister-in-law and brother*
>
> *Giuseppe and Sebastiana Delpopolo*
>
> *Again, holy resignation*

Giovanna and her husband, Alfio, sent their condolences from Buenos Aires. Giovanna was 14 years old when she last saw my grandparents before they emigrated in 1920. The letter appears to have been written by Alfio; I am not sure how much comfort it provided.

> *Dearest sister-in-law and sister we still have not got the courage to answer your letter of December 12 because of the sad and bad news of the loss of our dear brother-in-law such that it not only appears to be a dream but also, dear sister-in-law, I don't have the will to write because talking about it makes tears come to my eyes and I cannot write to tell you our pain and unhappiness at having lost the very best brother-in-law for being so affectionate towards all his relatives, despite his being so far away, as one can therefore never forget. Moreover, dear sister-in-law, I who write you cannot do so myself anymore because I no longer get satisfaction in correspondence since you don't know how to write. In fact, in the past it used to seem that we talked face to face as much when I received your letter as when you wrote us, so, dear sister-in-law and sister not only did we share the pain of a loss of your beloved husband who was the only comfort of your life but you also had the worry about being able to reply whether to us or to other relatives on account of your children not being able to write in Italian. So, dear sister-in-law and sister and nieces we all don't know how to speak to you to comfort you on the loss of our dear brother-in-law whom we will never forget. But in the meantime it is useless to think or to weep because the world was created like that for everyone. So, be as it may, there is nothing left to do but pray for him that he will be able to enter paradise and resign yourselves to destiny especially in the sudden case of how destiny came to be on the day 2-12 (December 2) never to be able to think of it especially since he did not feel ill when he last wrote us. Nothing else except that you receive fond kisses of comfort from all of us united, particularly you, sister-in-law and sister, yours affectionately*
>
> *Alfio and Giovanna*

My grandfather wrote most of the letters to the Delpopolo and Scafidi families, sometimes with the help of his neighbor, Domenica Cotrupi. He also taught his daughter, Concetta, how to read Italian so that she would be able to translate for her mother if he died first.

The black-bordered envelopes and letters that crossed the Atlantic from Sicily were deeply troubling for my grandparents, who suffered each loss without the support of an extended family. In 1939, nineteen years after leaving Sicily, Antonia received the dreaded news of her parents' deaths, just seven months apart. Her father was 71 years and her mother 69. The couple had been married for 43 years and, purportedly, both died in their vineyards.

Grief-stricken, my grandmother followed the mourning custom of her country, dressing fully in black (including stockings and apron) for the next three years. During that time, and again when he received the black-bordered notifications of his parents' deaths, Nanu respectfully wore a black cloth band around his upper arm to show his loss for the three-year mourning period.

*Nana in black mourning clothes,
one year after her husband's death.*

*Nana tying her robust tomato plants
in the backyard garden at 59 Cherry Street.*

# CHAPTER XII
# I REMEMBER NANA

*Tu ridi oje che jeu rido dumani.*
YOU LAUGH TODAY, FOR TOMORROW IT IS MY TURN TO LAUGH.

There was not a trace of the young Antonia Maria Delpopolo in the grandmotherly woman I came to know as Nana. While I outgrew her short, stout frame by the time I was nine years old, I do not recall a time when I felt more than a child in her presence.

Nana spoke in a soothing Sicilian dialect, which bore little resemblance to the classical Tuscan Italian, the language of Dante. I understood and loved her foreign sounding words. She understood English, but would not utter a syllable of it. When surprised, frustrated, or otherwise excited, she broke her usual reserve with arms lifted to the heavens and uttered the all-purpose expletive, "Madonna!"

It was to this modest, painfully shy woman that I turned for food and sympathy, both doled out at her kitchen table, in a room full of fragrances that I will never forget. She was my teacher and my Mother Confessor. Her wisdom was equal parts voodoo, Catholicism, and old-country customs, liberally mixed with a fear of the unknown and a haunting melancholy.

Her pessimistic mantra was *Ridi oggi; piangi domain*, "Laugh today; cry tomorrow," a sure-fire fix for a childish case of the giggles. Regrettably, Nana did not add a sprinkling of Taoist balance to her superstitious admonition with *Piangi oggi; ridi domain*, "Cry today; laugh tomorrow."

She also believed in omens, dream revelations, and the dreaded *il malocchio*, "the evil eye." To give "the evil eye," *guardar di malocchio*, was to place a curse on the object of your disfavor or, in more benign terms, to "shoot a look." She warned against the appearance of a snake and a friend in the same dream—a timely revelation that your friend was truly your enemy. Under no circumstances, let a bird fly into your house, for someone close was sure to die. To assure fair weather on your wedding day, hang rosary beads out the window.

At the same time, Nana maintained a special devotion to St. Anthony of Padua, praying before a plaster statue of him that she kept in her bedroom, perhaps recalling the Church of Sant' Antonio in Castiglione di Sicilia. She assured us not to worry when something came up missing. Instead, we turned to this Patron Saint of Lost and Found with the sing-song chant, "St. Anthony, St. Anthony, please come around. Something is lost and can not be found." Her favorite Madonna image was Our Lady of Carmel, whose framed print graced the living room.

In her role as family healer, Nana relied on the magical qualities of olive oil, which she rubbed on burns and rashes and dribbled warm into aching ears. She boiled it with parsley, garlic, and water as a cure for *acida*, a catchall term for a myriad of gastric upsets, which she was either warning to avoid (by not eating mayonnaise or food served in restaurants) or treating with a cup of the cooled concoction.

Nana made her own cough syrup, mixing honey and lemon with boiled chamomile blossoms. She strained the liquid and stored it in jars, ready to be doled out in tablespoon doses.

Among her medical miracles was the painless removal of slivers, thorns, and shards of glass. She covered the point of entry with a poultice of plantain leaves and milk-soaked bread wrapped tightly around the wound, which unfailingly drew the invasive object to the skin's surface. She also applied fresh plantain leaves to bee stings and insect bites to cessfully relieve the pain. (I later learned that the common green weed is an invaluable first-aid medicine with antibiotic qualities.)

Nana did not always overflow with the milk of human kindness. Regardless of her own timidity, she had a basic mistrust of "silent types" who were swiftly dismissed with, "Still water runs deep and dirty." While she was not alone in harboring a prejudice against the Irish, the fervor of her emotion became abundantly clear to me at age 14, when I introduced her to my first boyfriend whose nickname was Sweeney. After her usual show of food hospitality, Nana asked us to follow her outside, where she took a chicken from her coop, put its head on the chopping block, and raised an ax. The message that I was asked to translate for the new boyfriend went something like this, "If you do not take care of Sandy, I'll chop your head off too!" He was impressed.

Whatever the occasion, Nana's standard issue wardrobe consisted of cotton print dresses hemmed at mid-calf, covered by calico bib aprons that crisscrossed in the back, and serviceable black, laced shoes with a two-inch heel that replaced the button hook shoes she brought from Sicily.

Since she had not been given the opportunity to attend school in Castiglione di Sicilia, Nana could neither read nor write. All of her energy was harnessed to the tasks of caring for a family and the little world of house and garden, which she rarely left.

She cut her own patterns from newspapers laid out on the kitchen table to make clothes for herself and her four daughters—everything from flannel bloomers to the girls' tea-length dresses with drawstring book bags to match—all on a treadle sewing machine. She recycled her fifty-pound *Bridal Veil* flower sacks to make dishtowels, pillowcases, and basket liners. She learned to knit and outfitted her family in woolen hats, mittens, scarves, and sweaters—staples for a Vermont winter, the season that did not exist on the Mediterranean island of her childhood.

She gathered her four daughters around her for backyard summer schools of cross-stitch and embroidery, the signature handicraft of her Sicilian hometown and a major contributor to Castiglione di Sicilia's economy today. She enlisted Maria Zambone, her friend and upstairs tenant for a time, to teach her girls how to tat and smock. At the end of the summer, she marched her students, their summer creations in tow, to the Rutland Fair, where they earned blue ribbon premiums to buy their supplies for the new school year.

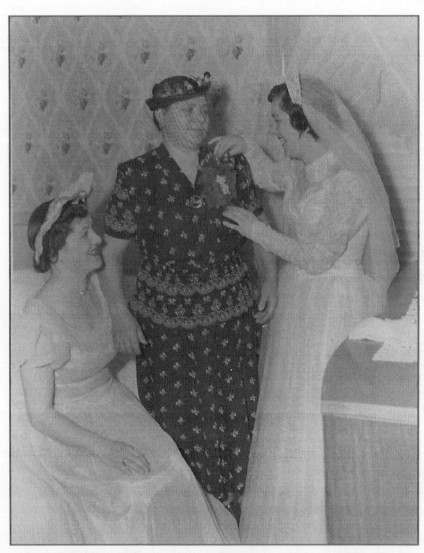

*April 16, 1951, Maria Scafidi's wedding day. Maria and her maid-of-honor, Concetta, took their reluctant mother shopping for her new hat at Milady's Millinery Shoppe on Rutland's Center Street.*

Nana made white soap for the bath and brown soap for the laundry. On Mondays, she boiled bed sheets, bath towels, and the family's clothing clean in a copper boiler heated on her coal-burning kitchen stove. She dried the laundry on clotheslines year round and spent Tuesdays pressing the freshly scented wash on a wooden ironing board.

She produced hard and soft cheeses from cows' and goats' milk, and root beer for picnics and special events. Every Monday and Thursday, she used a large galvanized washtub to make four big round loaves of bread, blessing each with a sign of the cross before baking. She raised chickens for their eggs and slaughtered them for meat. She made compost tea for her prize tomato plants in a covered barrel of chicken manure diluted with water at the edge of her backyard garden.

An experienced gardener, Nana resourcefully converted most of her tiny lawn to a carefully tended raised bed garden of tomatoes, basil, parsley, peppers and broccoli. She also worked alongside my grandfather in three much larger vegetable gardens on borrowed land, preserving whatever she could cultivate from this strange Vermont soil. Food was her passion, but her frugality was legendary.

In the summer, she sun-dried bowls of boiled, mashed, then strained tomatoes, moistened daily with olive oil, to make tomato paste. She packed the finished product, *conserva*, in jars topped with more olive oil, storing them in the back of her refrigerator to season winter soups and flavor her weekly batches of tomato sauce.

In the early fall, she parboiled peaches and pears in a backyard cauldron over an open flame, filling the bittersweet days of September with their unforgettably sweet fragrance. She canned the halved fruits, along with garden-fresh vegetables, dandelion greens, wild mushrooms and, sometimes, venison, lining the shelves of her root cellar with cheerful rows of jars.

The small wooden door to Nana's root cellar opened to an exotic "candy shop," that seems as magical in my memory as it did to my young eyes. The earthy scent of the dirt floor mingled with the smell of apples, ripening in bushels. Baskets and barrels of potatoes, carrots, and winter squash took shape as your eyes adjusted to the semi-darkness. The subdued summer brightness of blanched and boiled beans, beets, and corn formed a rainbow of color against the drab winter gray. But there was more to the root cellar than a roller coaster ride for the senses.

*Nana (56 years) and Sanda (7 years) at Blue Beach, Quonset Point, Rhode Island. The two spent a week with the family of Maria Valleroli whose husband was on shore duty at the Naval Base.*

It spelled safety and security, beyond the bomb shelter—a recent addition to our post World War II vocabulary.

Nana called me Sanda (pronounced sawn-daw). Much of the time, I was the apple of her Sicilian eye, but not always. In the Italian tradition of honoring first born, I inherited a venerable position in the family pecking order, as had my mother before me. But, strong-willed little girls slip often and fast from their pedestals.

I took my falls with Nana's ringing reprimand of *testa dura*. This rather unflattering way to describe a stubborn child was borrowed from the famously obstinate stonecutters of Carrara, whose dispositions were reportedly as hard as the marble they worked.

Still, no scolding was harsh enough to cover Nana's softhearted nature and the sweetness it carved into her face. Looming large in my memory is the summer day in 1964 when I was leaving Cherry Street to go away to school and it was time to say good-by to Nana. By then, she was widowed and living alone in the same house where she had raised her family, steadfastly fulfilling the duties of family matriarch.

I found her standing unusually still on her front lawn and realized that, in her intuitive way, Nana had been waiting for me to walk down the street. After a few cautionary remarks, she reached into her apron pocket and came out with a bundle of folded dollar bills, the $250.00 I was short for my first semester's tuition. It was a princely sum for both of us—squirreled away widow's benefits from her Social Security that saved me from a part-time job.

Bolstered by her daughters and grandchildren, or perhaps to bolster her daughters and grandchildren, Nana lived on without her husband for another 13 years. During that time it was she who quietly reigned over the special events of our lives, including her first grandchild's wedding and the birth of two great-grandchildren.

She and her Sicilian cookies were at the center of family birthday parties, First Holy Communions, Confirmations, and recitals. At her grandchildren's graduations, she was first in line for the inevitable round of picture taking that followed. Sporting her best dress, hat, and handbag, she held hands with the new graduate, solemnly boring into the camera in her Buddha-like pose.

I wonder. Were these sweet moments sweeter than what might have been in the place she left behind? Would the familiar cadence of her family and village life in Castiglione de Sicilia have been more satisfying than the vicarious joy she experienced as matriarch of an extended Italian-American family? Did the promise of a better future for her children and her children's children make her personal losses seem less painful? When her life ended, one month after her 74th birthday, was its outcome better or worse for the defining choice she made at age 22?

*And so our mothers and grandmothers have,*
*more often than not,*
*Anonymously handed on the creative spark,*
*the seed of the flower they themselves*
*never hoped to see –*
*or like a sealed letter*
*they could not plainly read.*

—Alice Walker

*Dressed in her widow's black, Nana (63 years) poses with her family in front of St. Peter's Church. Starting with back row, left to right: Assunta Cioffi, Concetta Miglis, Bill Miglis, and Maria Valleroli. Grandchildren in the front row, left to right: Frances Valleroli, Billy Miglis, Michelle Cioffi, Charron and Susan Valleroli.*

*Antonia and Francesco Scafidi on the front porch of their Cherry Street house (gray with dark green trim), which they carefully maintained and surrounded with flower gardens.*

## CHAPTER XIII
## THE NEIGHBORHOOD

*Cui nun senti a li cchiu granni, appenni li vertuli a mali banni.*
WHO FAILS TO LISTEN TO HIS ELDERS,
WILL HANG HIS KNAPSACK IN THE WRONG PLACE.

My grandparents and their paesani, along with several other Italian immigrants who put down roots in Rutland during the late 19th and early 20th centuries, lived in the southwestern section of the city, in a lowlands bordered by the railroad tracks and Otter Creek. The Sicilians and Italians followed the Irish immigrants, who settled in Rutland beginning in the 1820s and throughout the years of the potato famine.

West Street on the north, School Street on the south, Meadow Street on the west, and Forest Street on the east form the neighborhood boundaries. This several block district had its own markets and bakeries, barbers and cobblers, a playground, an ice-skating rink, and a lemon ice stand. It also had a three-story sweat shop, Dick's Dress Factory, where first and second generation women immigrants assembled piece work at rows of cutting tables and sewing machines.

The sweet taste of summer came packed in a small paper cup with a wooden spoon on top—Italian lemon ice. Joe Garafano, The Lemon Ice Man, happily served up homemade slush from a stand in front of his house at the junction of West and Meadow Streets, across from Marro's Store. We made the three-block pilgrimage every day that we could raise five cents. The price and the flavor held for two generations. Joe shared the following recipe with his Meadow Street neighbors, Phil (of Phil's Barbershop) and Mary Valleroli.

### Joe Garafano's Italian Lemon Ice

1 envelope unflavored gelatin softened in 1/4 cup cold water

4 cups water

1 cup sugar

juice from 3 lemons

Begin by adding the gelatin to 1/4 cup of cold water, setting the mixture aside to soften.

In a medium-size pan, bring 4 cups of water to a boil.

Add the sugar and let the mixture boil for five minutes.

Remove the syrup from the heat and stir in the lemon juice.

Add the softened gelatin, stirring until it dissolves.

Freeze the mixture in individual paper cups, ice cube trays, or a single container until firm (about 3 hours).

Serves four. Recipe is easily doubled, tripled…

Unlike the thousands of miles that separate me from my four grandchildren, there was only one house that separated me from my grandmother, and I saw her nearly every day of my early life. Our houses were on the same odd-numbered side of Cherry Street—Nana's at 59 and my family's at 63, on the corner of Franklin and Cherry. The sidewalks on Cherry Street were dirt paths cut through the grass, lined by a canopy of elm trees that were later lost to the devastating Dutch Elm disease which swept across New England in the late 1950s.

In between us lived the Stanziones, another family of Italian immigrants whose backyard garden nearly dwarfed their house. On summer nights, the unforgettable fragrance of fried zucchini drifted from their open windows along with the swelling notes of "Cherry Pink and Apple Blossom White," one of Butch Stanzione's favorite tunes. Butchie, the youngest of four sons, was simply practicing his trumpet. For the young girl on the other side of the prickly gooseberry patch that drew a line between our properties and social pecking order, it was the first brush with a teen idol.

On the front side of our house, the men of the neighborhood met under streetlights, as they had in their Sicilian villages, to smoke pipes and cigars, telling their stories to the night in soft murmurs. With the exception of my Hungarian father, the residents of Cherry Street were all Italian immigrants, with sing-song names like Sofia, Modica, Cotrupi, Padolecia, and Lemmo. The closing chorus of their *Buona Sita,* "Good Night," was the lullaby of my childhood, the last sound I heard before drifting off to sleep as the patriarchs returned to homes and obligations.

The women, my grandmother and her contemporaries, ruled over the neighborhood by day—watching from behind parted curtains, backyard gardens, and shady porches. Their telepathic network maintained an unspoken sense of order and daylight decorum—an informal Neighborhood Watch. The most one could expect of these thrifty conversationalists was a cordial *Buon Giorno,* "Good Morning," and a slight nod of the head.

The exception to their characteristic sparseness lived right across the street from us in the person of Dona Maniana, a stout and formidable woman who clearly did not like children. But there were five of us, the objects of her running stream of Sicilian slurs and scoldings for we knew not what. Strength in numbers greased our creativity and, in the long summers of childhood, we learned to fulfill Dona Maniana's prophecy of bad behavior. My favorite act of defiance was the "firecracker dance," which involved pulling handfuls of white berries from my mother's ornamental shrubs, throwing them to the ground, and jumping up and down on them to make popping sounds. My performance never failed to send Dona Maniana into convulsions of finger-pointing, fist-shaking fury.

A less threatening but more exotic neighbor, Rosa Sofia, lived on the corner of Cherry and Franklin Streets and did dramatic "evil eye" readings at her kitchen table. The supernatural belief in *il malocchio,* "the evil eye," was widely held by Sicilians, who brought with them to America a sense of fatalism and pessimism. They assumed that good fortune is fleeting and that prosperity invites envy, hollow compliments, and, in extreme cases of resentment, the casting of harmful spells.

Women of the neighborhood, left to right: Domenica Caggige, who traveled from Randazzo to Rutland with my grandmother, sharing the experience of the Atlantic crossing. Nana is seated next to her. Domenica Cotrupi, whose family owned the corner market at the end of Cherry Street and lived on Forest Street, was a close Scafidi family friend and my mother's Confirmation sponsor. Angelina Stanzione lived in the house between my family and my grandparents at 61 Cherry Street. Rosa Sofia lived across the street from my family on the corner of Cherry and Franklin. Nani Caggige, Domenica's daughter-in-law, married Raymond who, as a child, was cared for by my grandmother during their 19-day voyage from Sicily to Ellis Island.

If someone suspected that they had been cursed because of a string of bad luck or a sudden illness, they sought Rosa's indisputable diagnosis, which was based on an olive oil and water test to confirm *il malocchio* as the root cause. Rosa dipped her finger into a small dish of olive oil and then allowed three drops to fall into a nearby bowl of water. If the oil formed a circle on the water's surface it meant that the individual had been inflicted with *il malocchio*. If the water remained clear, however, the misfortune could not be blamed on a curse. Rosa's credibility was bolstered by her tenure in the Italian community. She and her husband, "Tony," were one of the first couples to emigrate from Sicily to Rutland in 1901.

NEIGHBORHOOD MARKETS

Giuseppe (Joseph) and Domenica (Monica) Cotrupi, and later Dominic (Mico), their son, and his wife, Linda, ran the corner store at the end of our street. Cotrupi's Market was one of five small stores on, or around the block from, Cherry Street, and we shopped there every day. Transactions—large and small—were charged and recorded with pencil in a thick, black ledger.

Only the children paid in hard-earned cash for their 10-cent comic books, eagerly anticipating the serialized escapades of Archie, Betty, Veronica, Reggie and Jughead, the main characters of Archie Comics. We often devoured the latest issue just outside Cotrupi's door, sitting on the curbside, racing from page to page. Another five cents could sweeten the experience with a cherry Popsicle, Fudgesicle, or an H-Bar—chocolate-coated orange sherbet or vanilla ice cream on a stick.

Just around the corner on Forest St. was Lemmo's Store, owned and operated by husband and wife team of Venera and Giatano, the brother of Rosario Lemmo, who lived across the street from my grandparents. The couple also emigrated from Randazzo. Their small market offered less variety than the others and did not carry meat or fish. Its primary attraction was as the daytime and weekend post for neighborhood men, who lined up on the ample window ledge.

A couple of doors down from Lemmo's stood the neighborhood fish emporium, the most exotic of all the markets. It was owned by Patsy Pattorti, who emigrated from Calabria, Italy. "Patsy kept vegetables on one side of the store and fruit on the other, but baccala was the main thing we sold and we sold it by the barrels," recalls my Aunt Jata, who went to work for Patsy at age 14.

A large platter of codfish, floating in a sauce of tomatoes, black olives, onions, potatoes, and carrots was the centerpiece of the Sicilian Christmas Eve table. I am sorry to say that the smelly process of soaking the dried fish and bringing it to the table took away any appetite I might have cultivated for the national dish.

The whole dried and salted codfish that hung from Patsy's store rafters, side by side with plucked chickens, were 12-15" long. To remove the salt, Nana soaked the dried fish for three days in a large pan of water set in her bathtub. Each rinse sent the fishy stench through the house clapboards into icy December air that preserved it for hours. The reek of baccala was compounded by the slow cooking in Sicilian kitchens, from one end of Cherry Street to the other. The Christmas smell that lingers in my memory, more than balsam, is my grandmother's baccala.

Christmas Day brought more Sicilian delights from Patsy, who had a local monopoly on calamari, sardines, and eels. He was not without competition for just across the way, on the corner of Forest and School Streets, the Bellomos, another couple from Randazzo, carried fish for the holidays. Mrs. Bellomo arrived in Rutland when she was 21 years old, and was much admired for her fine homemade sausage laced with hot pepper and *finocchio*, the ground fennel seed that imparted a distinctive flavor. Antoinette (probably Antonia) Bellomo and my grandmother shared the same recipe and made large batches together, allowing the seasonings to work their magic overnight before stuffing the mixture into casings.

But it was Patsy who lured the Sicilians back in between holidays for the rolls of cured and aged salami and provolone cheese, dangling on ropes from the ceiling. My Aunt Jata remembers that her father bought whole wheels of his favorite *formaggio al pepe*, a bland, white cow's milk cheese studded with peppercorns, which I later sought out and enjoyed in Catania's open food markets.

In the end, Bellomos had the staying power. The market has been a neighborhood landmark for 80 continuous years and the couple's son, Joe, carries on his mother's traditions of making sausage, sauce with meatballs, and Italian "grinders" stuffed with copocola, salami, provolone cheese, hot peppers, and onions.

## Nana's Baccala

1 pound dried salted cod fillet

2 tablespoons olive oil

1 medium size onion, chopped

1 32-ounce can of crushed tomatoes (Nana would use a jar of home-canned garden tomatoes)

1 handful of dried, black Sicilian olives reconstituted in a mixture of 1 teaspoon fennel seed, 1/8 tsp hot pepper, and 1 cup olive oil

2 cups water

salt, pepper, and hot pepper flakes, to taste

2 cups diced potato

1 cup diced carrot

10 springs Italian parsley, leaves only

The black olive mixture will add flavor to the stewed fish dish. Prepare it one week in advance by placing the olives in a jar with the olive oil, fennel seed, and hot pepper mixture. Strain the olives just before use.

Soak the dried codfish in a large pan of water for three days, changing the water three times per day. When the fish is tender, remove it from the water and prepare it for cooking by pulling off the skin and cutting the fillet into 2-inch squares.

Heat 2 tablespoons of oil in a heavy kettle, over low heat. Add the chopped onion, cooking until soft.

Add the crushed tomatoes and simmer the mixture for 30 minutes over low heat.

Add the codfish pieces and strained black olives to the tomato sauce. Continue simmering over low heat for an additional 30 minutes.

Add 2 cups of water and season, to taste, with salt, pepper, and hot pepper flakes.

Add the diced potatoes and carrots. Cook until the vegetables are tender and the fish is cooked through, adding water, as needed, to keep the fish covered in the process.

Transfer the baccala pieces from the cooking pot to a serving dish. Coarsely chop the parsley leaves and sprinkle them over the fish. Pour the hot tomato sauce and vegetables from the cooking pot over the fish and serve immediately.

# Nana's Sicilian Sausage

GET MARRIED, AND YOU ARE HAPPY FOR ONE DAY.
KILL A PIG, AND YOU ARE HAPPY FOR ONE YEAR.

- 8 pound lean pork shoulder, trimmed of rind and excess fat
- 2 tablespoons ground fennel seeds (start with whole fennel seeds and grind with mortar & pestle)
- 2 tablespoons salt
- 2 tablespoons pepper
- 1 tablespoon red pepper flakes, optional (add to make a hot sausage)
- 30 feet of sausage casing

Cube pork into one-inch squares.

Add fennel seed, salt, pepper, and optional pepper flakes to the meat mixture. Combine, cover, and refrigerate the mixture overnight to blend flavors.

Make sure that all of the ingredients, as well as the grinder or food processing blade used to grind the meat mixture, are very cold (prevents the meat and fat from forming a pate-like substance) before starting to make the sausage.

Make a double knot at one end of the casing before attaching the other end to the sausage-stuffing machine.

Twist or tie off sausage sections in six-inch segments to make links.

*Cheeses on display in Catania's open food market, October 2007.*

## The Neighborhood

Around the corner from Bellomo's, at the other end of School Street was Dellveneri's, the bakery we loved best for its small, five-cent paper bags of "crumbs"—shreds of crunchy bread crust that piled up under the slicing machine as the loaves pushed through. The brick ovens turned out honey-colored mounds of bread each morning before sunrise, along with rectangular pizzas in the tradition of Naples, once home to the Dellveneris.

My mother sent us off to the bakery early on Sunday mornings to beat the after-Mass rush. Our standing order was for "five doughs"—three for afternoon pizza and two for after church pizzies—fingers of bread dough, twisted like crullers, fried golden in oil, and rolled in sugar for a mouthwatering finish.

School Street opened onto Meadow and the neighborhood's epicurean center, Romano's Italian Pastry Shop, where at day's end customers could fill a brown grocery bag with whatever had not sold—thirty-five cents a bagful. The third Italian bakery, Mainolfi's, best known for its cinnamon sugar doughnuts, is now located on West Street.

The best place to buy penny candy was at Sherman's, the only non-Italian market in the neighborhood, on the Forest Street side of our block, just behind the cherry tree in our backyard. As close as the confection emporium of our dreams was, shopping expeditions were few and far between. Whenever my sister Judy and I had the opportunity, we stood before those long glass cases filled with Mary Janes, Squirrels, Swedish fish, Mexican hats, root beer barrels, licorice sugar babies, banana-flavored Bonamo Turkish Taffy, wax lips and coke-shaped wax bottles filled with colored sugar water, trying the storekeeper's patience with the weight of our decision-making.

Courtesy of the Rutland Historical Society.

CHAPTER XIV

OUR CHURCH

*Nun sputari in celu, ca te cada in faccia.*
DO NOT SPIT AGAINST HEAVEN, LEST IT FALL IN YOUR FACE.

The neighborhood's towering landmark, as much today as it was then, is St. Peter's Catholic Church. It was built on a "ledge" lot at the corner of Mechanic Street (now Convent Avenue) and Meadow Street, construction beginning in the summer of 1868. The Gothic-style structure was designed by Patrick C. Keeley, a well-known Catholic architect from Brooklyn, New York, credited with over 700 Catholic churches in his lifetime.

St. Peter's is constructed with stone quarried from the very lot upon which it stands by men of the parish, most of them Irish employees of the marble companies. The parishioners gave their time and used their own picks, shovels, and teams of horses to excavate enough blue-gray stone for the building's foundation and walls. Five years later, the church was completed and dedicated on Sunday, June 29, 1873, the Feast of Saints Peter and Paul. One of its crowning features was a 60' x 80' fresco of the "Last Judgment" rising above the altar at the front of the church. It incorporated 264 figures and, at the time, was one of the largest frescoes in the United States.

It took several years for the Italian immigrants of the neighborhood, who held church services in various rented halls (all of them called the Church of Our Mother of Sorrows) to reconcile with the Irish to form an integrated Catholic congregation. St. Peter's became the church where the children of the Italian-American immigrants and their children's children were baptized, confirmed, married, and mourned in funeral masses. This was the case with our family.

The interior of the church remained largely unchanged for 75 years until newly arrived pastor, Father Robert F. Joyce, undertook a significant renovation in 1948. This was the St. Peter's of my childhood—a place of ritual and repetition. The religious aura started in the vestibule, just inside the heavy wooden doors, where only the fragrance of Easter lilies overpowered the lingering scent of incense. Before entering the main sanctuary, we dipped our right hands into a font of sponge-soaked holy water to make the Sign of the Cross, a tribute to the Holy Trinity of God. The blessing begins with the right hand on forehead, *In the name of the Father*; the hand drops to mid-chest, *and of the Son*; moves to the left shoulder, *and of the Holy Ghost;* and crosses for the finish at the right shoulder with *Amen*.

The red leather-covered doors on the other side of the vestibule opened to vaulted ceilings and buff-colored walls decorated with biblical inscriptions, painted angels, and frescoes of heavenly scenes in rich colors and gold leaf. The unearthly light of stained glass windows closed out the world.

Adding to the solemnity of the semi-dark interior were fourteen scenes from the Passion of Christ, called Stations of the Cross, sunk into the church's sidewalls. The red shaded tableaux with bas-relief figures in ivory were imported from Munich, Germany. They encourage a spiritual pilgrimage—a meditative walk from station to station—to recall and atone for the suffering and death of Jesus Christ.

Father Joyce's renovation included three new altars made of Vermont marble and manufactured by the Vermont Marble Company. The main cream-colored altar had a contrasting backdrop of Roxbury Verde antique and carved oak panels, with a life-size sculpted wood statue of St. Peter in the center. Before entering our pews, we were expected to genuflect on the right knee, with heads bowed toward the holy presence at the front of the church.

It was to the devotional side altars that we came, outside of Sunday Mass, to pray for our special intentions. We brought alms—the saved coins and folded dollar bills deposited in slots beneath rows of candles in red or cobalt glass. No request was too small to be lifted to the heavens with candle smoke if presented with humility and faith. Uncertain young girls and weathered women of the parish flocked to the Lady altar on the

*Interior of St. Peter's Church after Father Joyce's renovations.
Courtesy of St. Peter's Church.*

right, where a sweet-faced Blessed Virgin Mary, the Holy Mother of God, was enshrined on a white marble altar with an elaborately carved blue cloud.

Four morning masses, at 6:00, 8:00, 9:30, and 11:00, were offered on Sundays. As many as 1,400 parishioners could pack into the oiled chestnut pews trimmed with black walnut, and the balcony could accommodate 150, plus the choir.

Mrs. Murphy, organist, conductor, and director, reigned supreme over the choir members and soloists who performed the classical church music and Gregorian chants. She taught us how to read sheet music, to harmonize, and to appreciate the sacred songs of the liturgy. I was a second alto in Mrs. Murphy's choir—a regular at the 9:30 Sunday morning mass, and a never-miss at her Tuesday, after-school rehearsal in the choir loft.

We followed the Mass in our missals, thick prayer books written in Latin, with English translations. Before Pope John XXIII's Second Vatican Council (1962-1965) changed the reading of the Mass to English, the service was said entirely in Latin.

The missals bulged with holy cards, devotional prayers and images created for the Catholic faithful since the 15th century. Our teaching nuns doled out the cards for academic achievement and good behavior. We collected and traded them like baseball cards, replenishing our supply at the Sisters of St. Joseph's Convent Store, which also carried blessed rosary beads, medals, scapulas, plaster statues, and religious books.

Father Robert F. Joyce and the two parish priests who assisted him lived next to the church with their housekeeper and cook in the stately St. Peter's Rectory, originally built and used as a school. The priests wore flowing liturgical vestments on the altar and alternated between long black frocks or black suits with starched stand-up collars when on the streets.

They presided over the ceremonial events of our lives and listened to the whispered litanies of our transgressions in Saturday afternoon confessionals, as we began, "Bless me, Father, for I have sinned." Best of all, they had the power to absolve us of all our wrong doing if we promised to recite the number of "Our Fathers" and "Hail Marys" they deemed commensurate with our crimes against God and our fellow man.

*Our Church*

What relief to leave the darkened chamber of the confessional box, where the priest was silhouetted behind a small screen window and you, the confessor, were on your knees. What a small price to pay for absolution—to push back the confessional's red velvet doors and kneel in the dimly lit church to say your penance. How bright the world seemed with a shiny, white soul, scrubbed cleaned by an Act of Contrition.

The church's influence extended beyond its walls to our homes and, especially, to our Catholic schools where the study of Religion held as much weight as Mathematics and English.

At the start of each school day, our classroom teachers led us in the recitation of prayers, along with the Pledge of Allegiance to the United States. Before we wrote our names on work papers, tests and reports, we were instructed to make a cross with the letters JMJ at the top of the page, to call upon the blessings of the Holy Family of Jesus, Mary, and Joseph. We did not attend school on the Catholic Church's Holy Days of Obligation, nor on the March 19th Feast Day of St. Joseph, husband of the Blessed Virgin Mary, for whom the order of our teaching nuns was named. That was their day to celebrate, even as it interrupted the solemn season of Lent.

The entire St. Peter's Parochial School body filed around the corner to the church for Stations of the Cross during Lent, monthly First Friday services honoring the Sacred Heart of Jesus, and for Benediction of the Blessed Sacrament, a devotional ceremony during which the Holy Eucharist is taken out of the tabernacle and exposed in a gold monstrance on the main altar. Our student congregation participated in the solemn service by singing verses from two Mediaeval Latin hymns written by St. Thomas Aquinas, the "Tantum ergo" and "O Salutaris Hostia." The Latin lyrics may have escaped us, but there is not a St. Peter's School graduate "of the times" for whom the melodies of these hymns are not deeply etched.

UNDER A FIG TREE

*TANTUM ERGO*

*Tantum ergo Sacramentum
Veneremur cernui:
Et antiquum documentum
Novo cedat ritui:
Praestet fides supplementum
Sensuum defectui.*

*Genitori, Genitoque
Laus et jubilatio,
Salus, honor, virtus quoque
Sit et benedictio:
Procedenti ab utroque
Compar sit laudatio.
Amen.*

*O SALUTARIS HOSTIA*

*O salutaris Hostia,
Quae caeli pandis ostium:
Bella premunt hostilia,
Da robur, fer auxilium.*

*Uni trinoque Domino
Sit sempiterna gloria,
Qui vitam sine termino
Nobis donet in patria.
Amen.*

Father Joyce, who presided over so many liturgical services, went on to become Bishop of Burlington, the religious leader for the Catholic Diocese of Vermont. He was a beloved priest for 67 years and bishop for 35, but for most of my years at St. Peter's Parochial, he was the popular parish pastor who entertained with parables at Friday afternoon school assemblies. Not unlike the simple stories with a single message that Jesus told to his followers, Father Joyce drew upon the animal kingdom adventures of his main character, "Froggy," to teach the lesson of responsibility, not only for our own salvation, but also for that of our fellow man. At the end of every story, regardless of the earthly and moral dilemmas that challenged Froggy, Father Joyce would ask in his Irish tenor,

*Reverend Robert F. Joyce,
6th pastor of St. Peter's Parish.
Photo courtesy of St. Peter's Church.*

"Now boys and girls, what would Froggy say?" In unison, we would shout back the memorable refrain that he taught us, "Don't go to heaven alone; take somebody with you."

In May, our school observed a month long devotion to Mary the Mother of God, a tradition believed to have originated in Italy and spread throughout the Roman Catholic world in the 19th century. Every classroom had a Mary, Queen of the May shrine, usually decorated with long-anticipated spring flowers and twirled strips of pink, white, and blue crepe paper cascading around a statue of the Blessed Virgin on a small altar. Our mothers sent in garden bouquets of iris, tulips, and heady lilacs that lulled us into mid-afternoon stupors. We added bunches of spring violets, red clover, and dandelion blossoms picked in vacant lots on the way to school.

Every day we sang traditional hymns such as "Tis the Month of Our Mother" and "Immaculate Mary," interspersed with "Hail Marys." All this in anticipation of the climactic event —the May Crowning—for which a girl in each classroom was selected to place a crown on the statue.

I was the lucky first-grader in Sister St. Justin's class chosen for the honor, which included carrying the crown on its cushion in a classroom processional of little girls dressed in white and boys in their Sunday best, singing "Oh Mary! We crown thee with blossoms today. Queen of the Angels, Queen of the May." My

*Photo of Sister St. Justin taken by the author in 1995, forty-five years after the May Crowning. Sister's habit had changed, but she had not.*

mother made the white satin covered pillow with pale blue ribbons and bows on the corners, which Sister Justin used for all of the May Crownings that followed in her long teaching career.

### QUEEN OF THE MAY
### (BRING FLOWERS OF THE RAREST)

*Bring flowers of the fairest*
*Bring flowers of the rarest*
*From garden and woodland*
*And hillside and vale*
*Our full hearts are swelling*
*Our glad voices telling*
*The praise of the loveliest*
*Rose of the vale.*

*Refrain:*
*Oh Mary! we crown thee with blossoms today*
*Queen of the Angels, Queen of the May*
*Oh Mary! we crown thee with blossoms today*
*Queen of the Angels, Queen of the May*

*Our voices ascending,*
*In harmony blending*
*Oh! Thus may our hearts turn*
*Dear Mother, to thee*
*Oh, Thus shall we prove thee*
*How truly we love thee*
*How dark without Mary*
*Life's journey would be*
*Refrain*

*O Virgin most tender*
*Our homage we render*
*Thy love and protection*
*Sweet Mother, to win*
*In danger defend us*
*In sorrow befriend us*
*And shield our hearts*
*From contagion and sin*
*Refrain*

*Of Mothers the dearest*
*Oh, wilt thou be nearest*
*When life with temptation*
*Is darkly replete*
*Forsake us, O never*
*Our hearts be they ever*
*As Pure as the lilies*
*We lay at thy feet*

## TIS THE MONTH OF OUR MOTHER

*'Tis the month of our Mother*
*The blessed and beautiful days,*
*When our lips and our spirits,*
*Are glowing with love and with praise.*

*Refrain:*
*All Hail! to thee, dear Mary.*
*the guardian of our way;*
*To the fairest of Queens,*
*Be the fairest of seasons, sweet May.*

*Oh! what peace to her children,*
*mid sorrows and trials to know,*
*that the love of their Mother,*
*Hath ever a solace for woe.*
*Refrain*

*And, what joy to the erring,*
*The sinful and sorrowful soul;*
*That a trust in her guidance,*
*Will lead to a glorious goal.*
*Refrain*

*Let us sing then, rejoicing,*
*That God hath so honored our race,*
*As to clothe with our nature,*
*Sweet Mary, the Mother of Grace.*
*Refrain*

### IMMACULATE MARY

*Immaculate Mary, your praises we sing;*
*You reign now in splendor with Jesus our King.*
*Ave, ave, ave, Maria! Ave, ave, Maria.*

*In heaven, the blessed your glory proclaim;*
*On earth we, your children, invoke your sweet name.*
*Ave, ave, ave, Maria! Ave, ave, Maria.*

*We pray for the Church, our true Mother on earth,*
*And beg you to watch o'er the land of our birth.*
*Ave, ave, ave, Maria! Ave, ave, Maria.*

Our Catholic neighborhood also greeted and welcomed the return of spring and the celebration of the Queen of the May with organized family devotionals at a different house each night of the month. A statue of Mary moved from the church to the living rooms of St. Peter's parishioners, who invited friends and neighbors to "say the rosary" with them and a parish priest in the early evening. Those who attended knelt to pray before simple tabletop shrines decorated with flowers.

At the end of the growing season, our thoughts returned to Mary with the feast of Our Lady of the Rosary on October 7th and a month-long devotion of the rosary. For St. Peter's students that meant a lunch period shortened by 15 minutes to accommodate a group recitation of the rosary in front of the school's outdoor shrine dedicated to the Holy Family.

Church, school, and home —the perfect triangle in two square blocks. What did it add up to? For some of us, "Why would I leave?" For others, "How could I stay?" Or, perhaps unconsciously and over time, "Now that I'm here, how do I find or replicate a semblance of this experience in my life?"

*The young eyes of Judy, Sandy, and Bobby Varga are focused on a statue of the Virgin Mary, at a neighborhood devotional held at the Manfredi home on Franklin Street in May 1953.*

*The teaching Sisters of Saint Joseph on the steps of Mount Saint Joseph Academy, "MSJ." Courtesy of the Sisters of Saint Joseph.*

# CHAPTER XV

# THE SISTERS OF ST. JOSEPH

*Ogni beni di Diu veni.*
EVERY GOOD THING COMES FROM GOD.

The good Sisters of Saint Joseph occupied the entire side of Convent Avenue, opposite the Church and rectory. Their four-story convent, flanked by a Catholic kindergarten and a high school academy, was where the sisters took in five year old fledglings and released them to the world, 13 years later, in the names of Jesus, Mary, and Joseph.

The first five sisters were recruited in 1873 from the Flushing, New York community of the Sisters of Saint Joseph to teach students enrolled for the fall term at St. Peter's School. Between 1873 and 1885, the school registered 325 to 375 children.

Construction of the convent was completed in 1882 and, three years later, the teaching sisters separated from the Flushing convent and established a Motherhouse in Rutland, becoming a recognized diocesan order of Vermont.

These quiet women, in floor-length black habits of heavy serge, a rope of big black rosary beads swaying from their waists, faces rimmed with starched white wimples, and hair concealed by long black veils, were revered members of the community for they taught the immigrants' children and grandchildren, preparing them for a better life as second and third generation Americans. And, what a wonderful education they provided, marching us through the years held to their high standards and the hopes of our parents and grandparents.

Their own lives were ones of sacrifice. In taking their religious order's solemn vows of poverty, chastity, and obedience, the sisters renounced the material world to serve God. They dedicated themselves to the education of youth and works of mercy. They promised to submit their will to the authority of the convent's Mother Superior. They traded their names for the names of the saints and became Sister Mary Clementine, Sister James Patrick, Sister Agnes Marie, Sister Mary Cephas, Sister Miriam Teresa, Sister John Joseph, and Sister Mary Emmanuel.

They gave up their parental home along with any prospect of a home of their own in return for a "consecrated life" in a community removed from the world and its pleasures. They forfeited daily interaction with family and friends for brief, scheduled visits in the convent parlor. On the day they took the "black veil" and adopted a nun's life, they also gave up their hair, which was shorn short forevermore.

That momentous day follows an apprenticeship period during which the nun-in-training-and-trial is called a postulate. Becoming a "Bride of Christ" involves the same rituals as a Catholic marriage ceremony, starting with a solemn mass in the presence of the other sisters and the postulate's family and friends in the convent chapel. The young woman enters in a white bridal gown, with flowers and veil, and receives a wedding ring which she will wear to her grave. After a wedding breakfast with bridal cake, she bids farewell to family and friends, exchanges bridal clothes for the somber religious habit of a novice and, with newly shorn hair, begins her religious life.

*The Sisters of St. Joseph*

This was also a life of "do not show" and "do not tell." We knew that many of these sisters were from Rutland families, but that was whispered information. In the course of my research I discovered that Sr. Mary Anthony, the strict but kind principal of St. Peter's School during most of my eight years there, was the daughter of Giuseppe and Gaetana Foti, with whom my grandparents stayed when they arrived from Randazzo and later shared many holidays. I also learned that Sr. Mary Anthony was my Aunt Mary's godmother. Because of strict convent rules, she was not allowed to attend my aunt's wedding at Saint Peter's Church, just across the street. Instead, she watched the comings and goings of the wedding party from her third floor convent window, and arranged to have a crucifix delivered to my grandparent's house as a wedding gift for the newlyweds.

*Three sisters from the Costello family of Rutland, Vermont entered the order of the Sisters of Saint Joseph and took the saints' names of: (left to right) Sister Mary Dolores, Sister St. Bernard, and Sister Mary St. Catherine. Courtesy of the Sisters of Saint Joseph.*

*Entrances to our Convent Kindergarten, with the Virgin Mary Grotto in the background, and Mount Saint Joseph Academy, May 2009.*

*Courtesy of the Sisters of Saint Joseph.*

*Courtesy of the Sisters of Saint Joseph.*

## The Sisters of St. Joseph

We could see the nuns walking the grounds behind the convent, saying their rosary, or sitting in the shaded gazebo reading, but we dared not look in their direction through the chain link fence as we walked down Meadow Street. When the door that separated the high school academy from the convent opened, we might catch a momentary glimpse of nuns on hands and knees, polishing the long marble floors of their living quarters, but we never spoke of it.

The sisters left the convent in twos, silently gliding through the neighborhood, as on a mission, with heads bowed. The one happy exception to this rule of solitude came when the convent doors opened in early morning, releasing the teaching sisters of St. Peter's Parochial, located just behind the church and the rectory on the corner of River and Meadow Streets.

Across the street their pupils were waiting for the privilege of walking by the sisters' sides as they rushed down the sidewalk, rosary beads swaying from their waists and clicking with every stride. We jockeyed for position, our spirits soaring with the rare opportunity of proximity to these larger-than-life women.

The routine was reversed at mid-day, when the sisters returned to the convent. The other children went home to lunch. I went to Nana's kitchen.

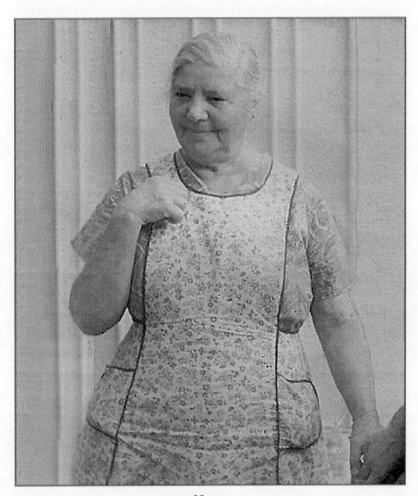

*Nana.*

## CHAPTER XVI

## OUR DAILY BREAD

*A cui ti po pigghiari chiddu chi hai, dacci chiddu chi t'addumanna.*
IF SOMEONE CAN TAKE WHATEVER YOU HAVE, GIVE THEM WHATEVER THEY ASK FOR.

Nana prepared our mid-day meal every day, but getting it to our table required the precision of a military drill team.

I wasted no time after the school's 11:25 a.m. lunch dismissal bell, taking the most direct route to my mother's kitchen door, whereupon she picked up the phone to alert Nana. I then exited the front door and walked down the street, skirting through Nana's back yard to her kitchen door, where she was already leaning out, holding a hot, white enamel soup pot with a rolled-up dishtowel on each handle, and wearing her smile of approval.

The pot was heavy, the smell divine, and Nana's daily warnings, delivered in Sicilian staccato as predictable as the pot's contents. *Sta' attendu, Sanda. Tiene le tavaglie. Non ti bruciare!* "Be careful, Sandy. Hold onto the dishtowels. Don't burn yourself!"

The menu of comfort food varied little day by day, year after year. As in Sicily where soup is the mainstay of *la cucina povera*, peasant's cuisine, simple ingredients are prepared repetitively and perfectly. Monday was my favorite, *lenticchi e pasta*, Ditalini with lentils served in a light brown broth. My sister, Judy, preferred Tuesday's pale yellow soup, *pasta con ciciadi*, Ditalini with chickpeas. Our younger brother, Bob, looked forward to Wednesday's *pasta e fagioli* (pronounced "pasta fazool") *Ditalini* with one of the many varieties of beans that my grandfather raised and dried on long sheets of canvas stretched across his back yard.

*Sacks of dried chickpeas and lentils, two staples of the Sicilian diet. Neighborhood market, Catania, October 2007.*

Thursday was a wild card—the daily special changing with the season and, one would hope, with Nana's whims. In the summer it might be manercia, a rich tomato-based soup, starring Swiss chard, chunks of Romano cheese and garlic. *Brodo di carne*, a beef broth served with vegetables and tiny pasta called Tubetini, alternated with chicken soup, *brodo di pollo*, in the winter months.

All of these rustic soups, with Italian names as numerous—minestra, brodo, zuppa, and minestrone—relied on ingredients that could be grown or produced at home or nearby, a testimony to the soup maker's ingenuity and frugality. Sicilians say, *Sette cose fa la zuppa*. "Soup does seven things." It relieves your hunger, quenches your thirst, fills your stomach, cleans your teeth, makes you sleep, helps you digest, and colors your cheeks.

Every Italian woman makes a signature tomato sauce with sacred nuances. Nana made her Sunday sauce and meatballs on Friday mornings and the "macaroni" test run was ours for lunch—fat Rigatoni noodles drenched in tomato sauce and served with a loaf of crusty Italian bread from Dellveneri's Bakery. For the main event, Nana served the sauce with long fettuccini noodles that she made early on Sunday mornings.

These heavily regional dishes were an art form in protein/carbohydrate balance long before "The Zone" and a proliferation of other 21st-century diets came along to teach Americans how to eat as well as my Sicilian ancestors. Still, by the time I was old enough for lunch dates, the exotic treats became the "American food," like gooey grilled cheese sandwiches and tuna melts on an English muffin that I sampled while visiting my school friends' homes.

No dish better illustrates the satisfying simplicity of the Sicilian diet than *Insalata Siciliana*—a lettuce-less salad of quartered garden tomatoes with basil, chopped garlic, and the standard dressing of olive oil, red wine vinegar, salt and pepper. It is served with hunks of a dry crusty bread for dipping, thus Nana's even more colloquial name for the high summer family favorite, *Bagna-Bagna* (Dip-Dip).

The following pages include handed-down recipes for Nana's weekly soup menu and tomato sauce.

## Monday's Lentiche e Pasta

1 cup lentils

3 cups water

1-2 clove(s) garlic, minced

2 tablespoons olive oil

2-4 tablespoons of fresh, chopped parsley (to taste)

salt & pepper to taste

hot pepper flakes, optional

1 1/2 cups of Ditalini pasta cooked in boiling water until al dente

In a medium saucepan combine the lentils and 3 cups of water, bringing the mixture to a boil.

Reduce the heat and simmer until the lentils are soft, adding water as needed to keep the lentils covered.

Add the garlic, olive oil, parsley, and seasonings, continuing to simmer until the flavors are blended.

Meanwhile, cook the Ditalini pasta in boiling water until al dente.

Drain the pasta and pour the lentil mixture over it. Serve immediately.

## Tuesday's Pasta Con Ciciadi

1 cup dried chickpeas (Nana dry-roasted chick peas on the top of her coal-burning cook stove.)

6-8 cups water

1-2 clove(s) garlic, minced

2 tablespoons olive oil

salt & pepper

fresh parsley, chopped, for garnish

1 1/2 cups Ditalini pasta

Rinse and sort the chickpeas, "garbanzos," before soaking them in 6-8 cups of water overnight.

Drain soak water and rinse the chickpeas in cold water.

Transfer chickpeas to a medium saucepan, with barely enough water to cover them. Maintain the water level (adding hot water, as needed) while the chickpeas simmer until tender.

When tender, add the olive oil, minced garlic, and salt & pepper, to taste. Continue to simmer until the flavors are blended.

Meanwhile, cook 1 1/2 cups of Ditalini pasta in boiling water for 6-7 minutes, until al dente.

Drain the pasta and pour the chickpea mixture over it. Garnish with parsley and serve immediately.

NOTE: The cooking process can be streamlined by starting with canned chickpeas, which eliminates steps 1-3.

## Wednesday's Pasta e Fagioli

1 small onion, chopped

2 cloves garlic, minced

2 tablespoons olive oil

6 ounce can tomato paste diluted with two cans of water, or substitute one or two 14.5 oz. cans of crushed tomatoes, depending on taste preference.

1/2 cup celery leaves, chopped

salt & pepper

2 tablespoons parsley, chopped (optional)

water or chicken broth

15 ounce can Cannellini beans, drained

1 1/2 cups of Ditalini pasta

Saute the onion and garlic until tender.

Add the tomato paste and 2 cans of water, or crushed tomatoes. Simmer for 15 minutes, and then add the celery leaves and parsley.

Cook the mixture over low heat for an hour, adding water or chicken broth, as needed.

Add the can of drained (and rinsed, depending on preference) Cannellini beans and simmer until the beans are warmed through.

Meanwhile, cook 1 1/2 cups of Ditalini pasta in boiling water for 6-7 minutes, until al dente. Drain the pasta and pour the bean mixture over it. Serve immediately.

## Brodo di Carne

- 2 pounds meaty beef shanks with bone, trimmed of excess fat
- 1 medium onion, peeled, or an equivalent amount of pearl onions, peeled
- 1 medium carrot, peeled
- 1 celery stalk with leafy top
- 3 sprigs parsley
- 1 can of Italian plum tomatoes, or 1 large fresh tomato
- salt & pepper
- 1 bay leaf, optional
- 1-2 cups Tubetini pasta

Bring a large kettle of warm water to a boil.

Add trimmed beef shanks and continue to boil, skimming fat from the water's surface.

When no more fat surfaces, drain and rinse the meat and bones, discarding the water.

Return the meat and bones to the pot and cover with cold water by 2 inches. Bring to a boil.

Reduce the heat and add the vegetables, parsley, and bay leaf (optional) to the pot.

Simmer gently, uncovered, for 1-2 hours. Skim top as necessary. Do not let the broth boil or it will be cloudy.

Strain the broth and refrigerate. When completely cold, remove fat from the top.

Remove the meat from the bones and add to the finished broth, along with salt & pepper to taste. Simmer.

Meanwhile, cook the Tubetini pasta in boiling water until al dente. Add to the beef broth and serve immediately.

## Brodo di Pollo

- 4 quarts water
- one 2 1/2 pound chicken, whole or cut in pieces, fat removed and washed
- 2 carrots, washed and cut in 2-inch pieces
- 2 onions, peeled and quartered
- 4 celery ribs, with tops, cut in 2-inch pieces
- 1 bay leaf
- 1 small bunch parsley, coarsely chopped
- salt & pepper, to taste
- 1-2 cups Ditalini pasta or rice, optional

Bring the water to boil in a large, 7-8 quart stockpot.

Add chicken and bring to boil, skimming fat from the water's surface.

After a five-minute boil, discard the water, and rinse the chicken to clean the meat and clarify the broth.

Return the chicken to a rinsed pot. Cover with 4 quarts fresh cold water.

Bring the water to a boil, skim off any remaining fat, and add the vegetables and herbs.

Reduce the heat and gently simmer for 3-4 hours, covering the pot halfway to prevent evaporation.

Season with salt & pepper the last 30 minutes of cooking time. Discard bay leaf.

Remove chicken from the pot, de-bone, and return to the broth and vegetables.

Serve immediately; addition of Ditalini or rice optional.

## Manercia

2 pounds Swiss chard, washed and drained

2 tablespoons olive oil

2-4 cloves coarsely chopped garlic, depending on taste

2 large ripe tomatoes, peeled and chopped, or an equivalent amount of crushed canned tomatoes

1/2 cup water

salt & pepper to taste

1/4 lb. Romano cheese, cubed

Warm the olive oil in a large soup pot.

Add the garlic and cook gently until golden.

Mash the tomatoes into the olive and garlic mixture.

Add 1/2 cup water; salt & pepper to taste. Simmer the mixture for 20 minutes.

Pack Swiss chard into pot, with cubes of Romano cheese in between the layers.

Cover the pot to allow the chard to steam, stirring the mixture from time to time.

Serve the saucy dish with crusty Italian bread when the chard is tender.

## Nana's Sunday Sauce with Meatballs

1 tablespoon olive oil

1 thick pork chop or three links of Italian sausage

2 quarts of peeled tomatoes (strained through a food mill) or two 28 oz. cans of Hunt's Tomatoes

1 six-ounce can of tomato paste diluted with a full can of water

2-4 cloves of garlic, depending on taste

1 teaspoon sugar (optional; Nana used to sweeten Vermont-grown tomatoes that were not as flavorful as those grown in Sicily.)

1/8 teaspoon of baking soda, to combat the tomatoes' acidity

1 bay leaf & 1 teaspoon basil

1/4 teaspoon fennel seeds (optional)

Heat the olive oil over moderate heat and brown the pork chop and/or sausages on all sides.

Add the tomatoes, tomato paste diluted with water, garlic, bay leaf, and sugar.

Bring the sauce mixture to a boil; stir in a pinch of baking soda, which will cause the mixture to bubble.

Simmer over low heat for 20 minutes.

Stir in the basil and fennel and continue to cook over low heat for 5 minutes.

Add the meatballs and slow cook for 3-4 hours, until the sauce thickens to hold its shape on a spoon.

## Meatballs

- 1 pound lean ground beef or a combination of pork and beef
- 1/2 cup seasoned breadcrumbs
- 1/2 cup grated Parmesan or Romano cheese
- 1 clove garlic, minced
- 1 tablespoon parsley
- 1/4 teaspoon pepper
- 1/4 teaspoon salt
- 1 teaspoon fennel (optional)
- 2 tablespoons of olive oil
- 1 egg

Mix all of the ingredients then shape piece the size of golf balls.

Bake on ungreased cookie sheets in 350° oven for 15 minutes. Turn and bake for an additional 15 minutes before adding to the sauce mixture. (The meatballs may also be fried in olive oil before being added to the sauce.)

*Nun c'e megghiu sarsa di la fami.*
THERE IS NO BETTER SAUCE THAN HUNGER.

*Antonia and Francesco under the hemlock tree they planted when they purchased their Cherry Street house in 1924.*

# CHAPTER XVII
# NANA'S CUCINA

*A ogni aceddu lu so nido e beddu.*
EVERY BIRD THINKS ITS OWN NEST BEAUTIFUL.

By today's standards, Nana's pale yellow kitchen was bare bones. Physically and functionally, it dominated the house by serving the communal needs of our three-generation family for over 50 years. This was Nana's world of ritual and tightly held traditions—a mixture of the familiar, the foreign, and the fascinating.

No kitchen memory looms larger than the first rite of Nana's day, which took place in front of a small, round mirror to the right of her back kitchen door. Predictably as sunrise, she ran a wet comb through her waist-length hair, first bending forward, sending the cascade to her knees. Moving deftly, her fingers twisted three plaits into a long, thin braid, which she draped over her left shoulder, finished and cinched with a rubber band. The full transformation took place when she coiled the braid into a tight little bun at the nape of her neck.

Over time, Nana's long tresses changed from dark chestnut, to a salt and pepper sprinkling, to gray, then white streaked with yellow highlights. The style never changed. For all of her life, she wore the classic *tuppo* of her Sicilian ancestors.

My grandfather built a small shelf underneath the mirror for Nana to keep her hairbrush and comb. On the other side of the mirror, in front of a large window that overlooked her back yard, was her favorite rocking chair. This is where she sat to knit, mend, and to watch the large flock of pigeons she religiously fed. A small door behind her chair opened to a cream colored pantry of floor-to-ceiling cupboards separated by work counters that ran along all three sides.

The one kitchen curiosity that defied Nana's bighearted disposition and fueled my inquisitiveness was a three-tiered corner shelf holding a display of elephants in brass, porcelain, jade, and ivory. She guarded this miniature menagerie with an uncharacteristic "Look but don't touch." While she never discussed the collection's origin or its personal relevance, the mystery began to unravel on my first visit to Catania when I learned that the elephant is patron animal of the province. Moreover, elephants with upturned trunks, as those in Nana's collection, are symbols of good luck. Since she did not add to the collection, she must have brought it with her from the island of secrets—yet another lost explanation.

*In the center of Catania's famous Piazza del Duomo is the city's most memorable monument, the smiling Fontana dell' Elefante (Fountain of the Elephant, 1736). The comical statue is the city's symbol and its citizens' favorite meeting place. Locally, the elephant with an upturned trunk is known as Liotru. The elephant is thought to have retained some ancient magical powers that help calm Mt. Etna's restlessness. October 2007.*

## I DOLCE

*Cosi amari, tenili cari*
*Cosi duci, tneili 'nchiusi.*
LOOK AFTER SOUR THINGS CAREFULLY,
KEEP SWEET THINGS LOCKED UP.

There were no cupboards in Nana's kitchen. The long rectangular table covered in bright colored oilcloth was where she rolled out and cut pasta dough, kneaded bread, and prepared the pastries that were her specialty. Penny-pinching and practicality were put aside when it came to marking the special occasions of our lives. Nana was happy to indulge in the one culinary excess for which her homeland is celebrated—*i dolce*, its desserts.

Some food historians think that pastry making was invented in Sicily. In his 1971 edition of "The Food of Italy," author Waverley Root attributes the Sicilian sweet tooth to the Saracens (Muslims) who took control of the island in the 8th century, establishing their fine flaky pastry tradition wherever they invaded. Centuries later, the long, sweet history of Sicilian pastries remains tangled in the island's rituals and religious practices. While the recipes vary from region to region, village to village, and even from family to family, all of the pastries are universally linked to an ancient legend, the celebration of a particular feast, or a saint's day.

The familiar legend of Persephone and Demeter, generally associated with Greek mythology, actually has its origins with the Siculi, an ancient cult already established in Sicily when the Greeks arrived. One of today's most important Sicilian festivals, the March 19th celebration of Saint Joseph's Day, replaced the March feast of Demeter, which celebrated the arrival of Sicily's early spring. At the other end of the growing cycle, Persephone's annual descent into the underworld corresponds with the early December festival of *Santa Lucia*, Saint Lucy, the Sicilian virgin martyr. The ritual of eating certain sweets, many created in convents and monasteries, remains an honored part of the devout observance of these and other saint's days.

The pastry of religious sanctity in our family is the *gennet*, a dense lemony cookie drizzled with lemon icing and colored sprinkles. Nana's *gennets* made their appearance at Easter and Christmas, but they also showed up on "cookie trays" (large mounds of assorted cookies) prepared for family weddings and reunions of all sorts.

There are as many spellings of the cookie's name as there are pastry chefs in the family. However, none of these spellings helped me find information about the gennets' origin or celebratory association until I discovered nearly perfectly matched ingredients in two recipes for Aunt Irma's Easter Egg Biscuits (*Biscotti di Pasqua Alla Zia Irma*) and Lemon-Glazed Egg Biscuits (*Frolli di Uova*) in Nancy Verde Barr's "We Called It Macaroni: An American Heritage of Southern Italian Cooking."

Aunt Irma's Easter Egg Biscuits, with proportionately identical ingredients to my grandmother's *gennets*, are made with pencil-thin strips of six-inch-long ropes of pastry dough that are knotted "to simulate arms crossed over the chest in prayer," in the same fashion that Nana made her snail-shaped cookies. Pastries knotted like these are thought to have ancient religious origins.

The Lemon-Glazed Egg Biscuits, which were originally associated with Lent and Easter, fall into the category of drop cookies and include ricotta cheese to help them keep longer.

The even bigger breakthrough came with a visit to the Italian neighborhood in Boston's North End, where I encountered Giovanni Piccarello, the owner of Modern Pastry on Hanover Street. Giovanni, whose uncle opened the shop in 1931, has been its owner/pastry chef for the past 60 years. When I described the ingredients of Nana's *gennets*, he resolved the long-time spelling dilemma with a one-word exclamation, "*Anginetti!*," which is the classic Easter cookie of southern Italy.

Armed with this new information, I returned to the Internet and found several variations of recipes for *Anginetti*, also referred to as *Anginette* Cookies, Italian Iced Lemon Cookies, Rosettes, and Italian Lemon Drop Cookies, thus confirming the penchant of every Sicilian village to create and name its own version of the classic sweet.

In some Sicilian pastry recipes, including those for *anginetti*, the stronger essence of anise oil is substituted for lemon. The rival flavorings reflect the different races and cultures that have occupied Sicily, each leaving its lasting imprint on regional and local specialties. While lemon trees are ubiquitous on much of the island (ninety percent of Italy's lemons are grown in Sicily), the tradition of using anise seed as a flavoring can be traced to the Arabs who introduced its cultivation to Sicily during the early ninth century.

*Gennet* or *Anginetti*—just the sight of these cheerful little cookies evokes Easter morning in Nana's kitchen, circa 1950s. Following 9:30 High Mass at St. Peter's Church, we arrived at Nana's famished (having fasted from the night before to receive Holy Communion) and full of anticipation for one of her Easter egg baskets. Nana made the basket with *gennet* cookie dough, fashioned in the shape of a chicken, with a well in the center to hold an uncooked egg. She sculpted the front of the basket to form a chicken's head and pinched the opposite side to create upturned tail feathers. The egg was held in place by two strands of dough in the form of a cross and the entire creation was covered in colored sprinkles before baking. Nana pulled the egg baskets from her big cook stove oven just as we arrived from church. Heaven—and very appropriately so—on the feast of the Resurrection!

While we grandchildren feasted on warm *gennets* and hard-boiled eggs, our parents joined us around the kitchen table for a "grown-up" accompaniment to the Easter pastries—strong black coffee served with short glasses of anisette, an anise-flavored sweet liqueur reserved for special occasions.

Nana's spicy molasses cookie, the *Mussetti*, is another example of a localized dessert with similar ingredients of a Neapolitan pastry associated with the Lenten season and the dark winter months before the arrival of spring. The biscotti-shaped *Mussetti*, with its dry, dense, and chewy texture, is often dipped in coffee to soften.

The *Mussetti* and its not-too-distant relative, the Anise Bar, sometimes referred to as white *Mussetti*, were staples of Nana's Christmas and Easter cookie trays. Both of these tasty cookies are baked in loaves, cooled, and sliced on the diagonal to create individual cookie bars. Unlike traditional biscotti, they do not require a second baking to bring out their flavor.

Probably the best known of Sicilian desserts are *cannoli*, crispy tubular shaped pastries that are deep fried, then filled with a sweet creamy mixture. This is the one "Italian" pastry that indisputably bears the stamp of Sicilian authenticity.

Some culinary historians trace the origin of the *cannoli* to pre-Christian times and their shape to the island's ancient and mysterious stone steles of magical or religious importance. *Cannoli* inherited the steles' connotation of fertility symbols, and were served at weddings to insure fruitfulness to a new family.

Others credit the origin of the *cannoli* to the region around Palermo during the time of Arab occupation, while still others believe that the pastry's roots are in the Middle Ages. Most agree that, in "recent" history, *cannoli* were made for the *Carnevale* which, like Mardi Gras, is a festival that takes place on "Fat Tuesday," the day preceding the start of the Lenten season on "Ash Wednesday." Over time, the pastry's symbolic association with fertility evolved to an association with Easter, the Christian feast of rebirth.

Today, *cannoli* are made for any joyful occasion and are a year-round staple in Italian pastry shops. The fillings and flavoring vary as much as dimensions of the shells—from fist-sized offerings to the slender finger-like, *cannulicchi*, which I enjoyed on my visit to the historic town of Enna in the island's mountainous interior.

In Sicily, sweetened ricotta cheese was used to fill the shells since *Carnevale* is the time when sheep are grazing in their spring pastures and producing an abundance of milk for cheese production. Now, filling preferences have strayed from the classic ricotta to include sweetened mascarpone, custards, and creams—even ice cream.

Nana reserved *cannoli* making for Easter and Christmas, using four-inch sections of dried sugar cane stalk, in classic Sicilian style, to form the pastry. She filled the *cannoli* shells with a mixture of sweetened ricotta cheese, candied fruit, and pistachio nuts. With changing tastes, candied fruit and nuts are now infrequently used in the *cannoli* filling. Chocolate chips, however, are in!

## Nana's Gennets (Anginetti)
*from her daughter, Concetta Scafidi Miglis*

1 cup butter, melted

1 cup sugar

6 eggs

1 cup milk

1 bottle (1 oz.) pure lemon extract

5 cups flour (may add another 1/2 – 1 cup flour to reach the desired consistency)

6 teaspoons baking powder

pinch of salt

Whisk together the melted butter, sugar, eggs, and milk until there are just a few bumps left. Mix in the lemon extract.

Sift together the flour, baking powder, and salt.

Gradually add the sifted dry ingredients to the wet mixture to form a moist dough.

Knead the dough on a lightly floured board until it is no longer sticky, adding another 1/2 – 1 cup flour, if needed.

Shape the dough into a large loaf, moving it to the back of the floured board.

Divide the loaf into 6 or 7 sections.

Roll one section at a time into long logs, approximately one inch in diameter (the size of a quarter).

Cut the logs at six-inch intervals.

To give the genet its classic look, pick up one end of a six-inch section of log with your right hand, pressing it against the third finger of the left hand with the left thumb holding it in place.

Coil the roll around the tip of your third finger three times, in a counter-clockwise motion, tucking the opposite end of the roll down the hole at your fingertip to create a snail shape.

Bake on parchment paper-lined cookie sheets, in a 375° oven for seven minutes until the tips and bottoms of the cookies are golden. Yields 65.

Cool completely, frost, and top with colored sprinkles (optional).

ICING:

 4 cups confectioner's sugar

 5 tablespoons water

 2 teaspoons lemon extract

In electric mixer, beat all of the ingredients until smooth, adding more water, if necessary, to reach the desired consistency.

Dip the tops of the cookies into the icing, allowing the icing to drip down over the sides of the cookies.

Top with sprinkles (optional).

Dry the frosted cookies on wire cooling racks. Store in an airtight container.

## Gennets (Anginetti) with Ricotta
*a family recipe contributed by Mary Spine Valleroli*

5 cups flour

3/4 tablespoon baking soda

1 tablespoon baking powder

1 teaspoon salt

2 8-ounce sticks butter

2 cups sugar

2 1/2 bottles (1 oz.) pure lemon extract

3 eggs

2 cups ricotta cheese

ICING:

6 cups confectioner's sugar

1/2 cup water

2 teaspoons lemon extract

Sift together the flour, baking soda, baking powder and salt; set aside.

Cream the butter and sugar until light and fluffy. Beat in the lemon extract, then the eggs one at a time.

Slowly add the sifted dry ingredients, mixing until blended.

Mix in the ricotta cheese. Dough will be soft and sticky.

Cover and chill for at least two hours, if not overnight.

Preheat the oven to 350° and line two large baking sheets with parchment paper.

Drop the gennets by heaping teaspoonful onto the lined cookie sheets. Or, flour hands and roll a teaspoonful of dough into a ball and twist the top to make a little snail peak.

Bake for 10-12 minutes, or until firm and lightly golden. Yield: 75-80.

Cool, frost, and top with colored sprinkles (optional).

ICING:

In electric mixer, beat all of the ingredients until smooth.

Dip the tops of the cookies into the icing, allowing the icing to drip down over the sides of the cookies.

Top with sprinkles (optional).

Dry the frosted cookies on wire cooling racks. Store in an airtight container.

# Nana's Mussetti
*from her daughter, Concetta Scafidi Miglis*

6 cups flour (may need to add another 1/4 – 1/2 cup)

2 teaspoon baking soda

1 teaspoon baking powder

1/2 teaspoon salt

1/4 teaspoon pepper

1/4 teaspoon cinnamon

1/4 teaspoon ginger

1 cup sugar

1 egg

1/4 cup oil

1 cup molasses

1 cup brewed coffee, warm

1 tablespoon orange zest

1 cup Spanish peanuts (without skins) or walnuts

Sift the flour, baking powder, baking soda, salt, pepper, cinnamon, and ginger into a large mixing bowl. Set the dry mixture aside.

Beat the sugar, egg, and oil until thoroughly mixed.

Add the molasses, warm coffee, and orange zest to the other wet ingredients.

Gradually stir in the dry mixture and nuts, turning the bowl and working from the outside toward the center.

When the dough is evenly mixed, scrape it onto a lightly floured work surface and divide it into five equal pieces.

Form each piece into a 12" x 2" long loaf. If the dough is too soft to work with, you may need to add 1/4 - 1/2 cup of flour.

Cover and refrigerate the dough for 1-2 hours.

Transfer to a parchment-covered baking sheet and bake in a 350° preheated oven for 15-20 minutes, or until the top of the loaf cracks.

Cool and slice diagonally, at one-half inch intervals, into bars.

## Nana's Anise Bars
### from her daughter, Concetta Scafidi Miglis

1 heaping cup sugar

1 cup golden raisins

1 cup mixed candied citrus fruit

1 cup pignoli or walnuts

1/2 bottle (1 fl. oz.) pure anise extract or one bottle (.125 fl. oz.) of anise oil

1 1/4 cup milk (heat and cool)

12 tablespoons butter

4 eggs

5 cups sifted flour

4 teaspoons baking powder

1/8 teaspoon salt (optional)

1/2 teaspoon vanilla

2 tablespoons of water

Mix the sugar, raisins, candied fruit, nuts, and anise flavoring together. Cover and set aside for 2 hours.

Combine and gently warm the milk and butter. Allow the mixture to cool.

Pour the wet mixture over the other ingredients.

After beating the four eggs, pour them over the other ingredients. Combine well.

Sift the flour, baking powder, and salt together and add, one cup at a time, to the wet mixture.

Turn the dough onto a floured board and knead until the dough no longer sticks. (You may have to add 1/4 – 1/2 cup more flour).

Divide the dough into 4 or 5 equal pieces.

On a lightly floured surface, roll each piece into 13" football-shaped loaves.

Place loaves on parchment covered sheets.

Brush the loaves with 1/2 teaspoon of vanilla diluted with 2 tablespoons of water and top with colored sprinkles.

Bake in a 375" oven for 20-25 minutes, until the loaf begins to split on top and brown on the bottom.

Cool completely before slicing on the diagonal, at one-half inch intervals, into bars.

## Nana's Cannoli
*from her daughter, Concetta Scafidi Miglis*

SHELLS:

    3 cups flour

    1/4 teaspoon cinnamon

    pinch of salt

    3 tablespoons melted butter or Crisco (Nana used lard.)

    3 eggs

    4 tablespoons water

    2 tablespoons white vinegar

    1-2 beaten egg whites

    vegetable oil for deep-frying

In a medium mixing bowl, combine flour, cinnamon, and salt.

Add melted butter or Crisco.

In a small bowl, beat the eggs with the water; stir in the vinegar.

Combine all the ingredients. Turn out dough onto a lightly floured surface. Knead until well-mixed (approximately 5 minutes).

Wrap the dough in wax paper and refrigerate for 2 to 3 hours.

Cut the dough into four sections for easier handling.

On a lightly floured board, roll out each quarter of dough until very thin.

Using a cookie cutter or rim of a glass, cut dough into 4-inch rounds.

Wrap each round tightly around a cannoli tube, carefully sealing the edges together with beaten egg white. Press the edges together.

Fry in hot vegetable oil (360°) until golden brown, turning often with a slotted spoon.

Remove from the oil and drain on absorbent paper.

Cool and gently twist tube to remove the shell form.

Cool completely before filling.

## FILLING

- 3 pounds Ricotta cheese
- 1 cup sugar
- 2 tsp vanilla
- 1/2 cup mixed candied fruit
- 1/2 cup pistachio nuts

The night before making the cannoli, place the ricotta cheese on two linen dishtowels and tightly roll, securing the ends of the towels before refrigerating the ricotta overnight to drain water from the cheese.

The next morning, in a medium mixing bowl combine the ricotta with the other filling ingredients Refrigerate until ready to use.

Fill shells just before serving. Sprinkle with confectioner's sugar.

*Francesco Paolo Scafidi*

*"Observe immigrants not as they come travel-wan up the gangplank nor as they issue toil-begrimed from the pit's mouth or mill gate, but in their gatherings, washed, combed, and in their Sunday best."*
—*E. A. Ross, Sociologist, 1914*

CHAPTER XVIII

MAKING A LIVING...MAKING A LIFE

*Lu surci ci dici all nuci, "Dumani temp che ti spertusso."*
THE MOUSE SAYS TO THE NUT, "GIVE ME TIME AND I'LL OPEN YOU."

When my grandfather returned to Rutland in September 1920, the marble industry and the businesses that supported it were booming and hiring. There is no concealing his pluck and determination to get on with this new American life in the studio portrait taken at that time.

Where to begin? He took the most familiar route and followed many of his fellow countrymen to Howe Scale, a foundry and manufacturing facility that operated nine hours a day, six days a week.

On my mother's birth certificate, filed April 23, 1921, his occupation is stated as "Molder's Helper"—a foundry worker. His hire may have been related to the 1921 walkout initiated by the molders over an hourly wage dispute during one of the most volatile periods in the company's history.

I found Frongro Scaffeedo and Frongo Scaffeedo listed as employees of the Howe Scale Company in annual editions of the *Rutland Directory*, 1922 through 1925. The home addresses for Frongro and Frogo match all three places Frank and Antoinette Scafidi lived from the time of their arrival in 1920, confirming yet more creative misspellings of the family name. Ten years later, the 1930 census indicates that Frank Scafidi progressed to a Howe Scale "Molder," a more skilled foundry job at the front end of the casting process.

For 106 years, Howe Scale manufactured a full line of practical and innovative weighing devices—some gigantic enough to weigh railroad cars and canal boats. The company became world-renowned by earning several awards at fairs and competitions, including the gold, silver, and bronze metals at the 1867 Paris Exhibition.

In 1873, Howe Scale moved to Rutland from nearby Brandon where the business had operated since 1857. To take advantage of the city's rail connection, its new foundry and sprawling manufacturing facilities were tucked into an angle of land bordered by Rutland's railroad tracks where they branched east and west.

All of my grandfather's neighbors—Giuseppe Caggagi (Caggige), Rosario Lemmo, John Camardi, Salvatore Anzalone, Anthony Sofia, and Domenic Panarella—are listed in the *Rutland Directory* as employees of the Howe Scale Company during the 1920s. At the time they lived in a cluster of odd-numbered houses on one side of Spruce Street, which extended north of the River Street Bridge. The resettlement community appears on a 1925 spatial map of the city near the Rutland Railroad Round House, a large building for servicing steam locomotives and allowing them to change direction on its massive turntable. When the railroad expanded, the houses were moved or torn down and the northern end of Spruce Street disappeared from the city map. In this year's late winter snowmelt, I was surprised to discover a well-lit recreational path where the neighborhood once stood.

My mother's birth certificate lists the Scafidi residence as 69.5 Spruce Street, a duplex previously occupied by two other young Sicilian families who came to Rutland in 1912. By the time their second daughter, Concetta, was born in December 1922, the Scafidis had moved to 79 Spruce Street.

Two years later my grandfather, in partnership with Luigi Cala who also emigrated from Randazzo, purchased a large two-family house in the heart of Rutland's Italian neighborhood. The $4,000.00 property at 59 Cherry Street was transferred from Nicholas and Margaret Howley on June 4, 1924, five years before the start of the Great Depression.

The 1930 census indicates that Luigi (44 years old), Anna (36 years old), Constance (two years and six months old), and Louis (one year and one month old) lived in an upstairs apartment, while Frank (43 years old), Antonia (33 years old), Veronica (nine years old), Concetta (eight years old), Mary (six years old), and Alice (three years and five months old) occupied the first floor.

Fifteen years later, my grandfather bought out Luigi Cala's share of the house with the help of a short-term loan of $2,000 from Giuseppe Cotrupi who owned Cherry Street's corner market. The deed was transferred to the joint ownership of Frank and Antonia Scafidi on May 9, 1939, with their eldest daughter, 18-year-old Veronica, as witness. During this period, there was a flurry of activity in transferring and receiving funds from an account my grandfather maintained with the Postal Savings Bank in Sicily. The cross-Atlantic negotiations were conducted through Italy's Ministry of Communications.

At this time he was in his third year of employment for Kinsman & Mills, Inc., designers and builders of marble and granite memorials. The business was established in 1881 and located on Rutland's West Street.

City records indicate that Frank Scafidi left Howe Scale sometime after 1932, probably a victim of the Great Depression. He found employment through the Works Projects Administration (WPA), the New Deal Agency created by President Franklin Delano Roosevelt to provide 3.5 million jobs for unemployed workers (16 to 65 years of age) until the economy recovered. Congress appropriated funds for an annual worker salary of $1,200 for a 30-hour workweek. Anyone who needed a job was eligible.

In Rutland, WPA jobs to repair and maintain roads became available in the city's Public Works Department. From the time he left Howe Scale until he began working at Kinsman & Mills in 1936, my grandfather supported his family through this local road project and whatever odd jobs he could find.

From 1940 to 1945, he worked for The Clarendon & Pittsford Railroad, a standard gauge line developed between 1886 and 1918 by the Vermont Marble Company to haul stone from their quarries to processing plants.

The Summer 1981 issue (Volume XI No. 3) of the Rutland Historical Society *Quarterly* that features The Clarendon & Pittsford Railroad

*Vintage postcard, "Marble Quarry, Rutland, VT," No. 9411.
The Metropolitan News Co., Boston, MA and Germany.*

notes that all of the locomotive engines were named for directors of the marble company. The railroad's lines "operated from Florence (at the north end) and Hollister Quarry White Pigment Corporation plant and Loveland Quarry to Proctor and Center Rutland, with a branch line operating to the Central Vermont Public Service Corporation generating plant in Rutland. Another line went from Center Rutland to West Rutland, making the total distance 15.7 miles."

My grandfather was part of a crew that maintained and repaired a portion of the railroad track. He worked alongside his foreman, Frank Valleroli, and Frank's son, Emanuel, who would later earn the rank of Chief Petty Officer in the United States Navy and marry his former coworker's third daughter, Mary Scafidi.

After five years of working outdoors year-round, Frank Scafidi was probably ready to come in from the elements. He secured a position at the foundry of another internationally recognized business, the Patch-Wegner Company on Rutland's Railroad Street. In 1891, Fred Patch and his two partners, George T. and Newman K. Chaffee, purchased the foundry and machine shop that had been in continuous operation on that site since 1859. The previous business, Mansfield and Stimson, manufactured machinery for marble work, slate work, and lumber mills. Under Fred Patch's management, the company produced derricks, gang saws, overhead cranes, and other industrial machinery to support the accelerated growth of the Rutland area's marble industry.

By 1927, when it acquired the Julius Wegner Machine Works of Astoria, New York, F. R. Patch and Company was the largest marble machine company in the country, perhaps in the world. Under the changed name of the Patch-Wegner Company, Inc., the business continued to produce stone-working machinery for every state in the nation and several overseas markets until it closed in 1976.

The memories I have of my grandfather are from his years at Patch-Wegner, 1945 to 1956. He worked until he was 69 years old, enjoyed one year of retirement on his $1,020 Social Security income, and died the next. I suspect that he was worn out by the piled-up years of physical labor, the high price tag of his American dream. In Sicily, his father lived to be 86 and his older brother, Salvatore, who returned to the island's agro-lifestyle after a ten-year stint in Rutland, lived to be 88.

*Nanu in retirement, six months before his death.
His grandson, Billy Miglis, is on the swing
in the backyard of my grandparents' home.*

Like the majority of his immigrant neighbors, my grandfather never learned to drive. The route he walked was small and repetitive, suiting the simple rhythm of his life. It took him to his work, the homes of his friends and daughters, the nearby markets and downtown merchants, the Grand Theatre where he enjoyed Saturday afternoon cowboy serials, social events in the Italian community, and to his beloved gardens.

I recall seeing him walk home from Patch-Wegner in the late afternoon, with his blue agate-ware lunch pail, wearing the soot of the day—whistling, often to the melody of *Cinquecento*, a stirring song about 500 young Italian Army recruits going off to war.

Fastidious by nature, he immediately bathed, changed into crisp clean clothes, and refreshed himself with ice-cold lemonade that my grandmother prepared for him in a glass hobnail pitcher that I now have.

A man of great discipline and little excess, he allowed himself one unfiltered Camel cigarette a day which he smoked after the evening meal. In the summertime, he combined the indulgence with a contented stroll around his gardens.

My grandfather loved Italian music and his cabinet radio, which occupied a venerable position in the infrequently used living room—except, that is, for Sundays. The entire family gathered around the wooden console from 11:00 a.m. until noon for the *Italian Hour*, which was preceded by the *Polish Hour* on Rutland station WHWB. Italian host, Pasquale Valente, brought his personal record collection to the station and encouraged call-in requests from listeners.

Nanu was a frequent caller, often requesting the stirring *Santa Lucia*, Julius LaRosa's rendition of *O Sole Mio*, and a Sicilian folksong about courtship and marriage called *E la Luna Mezzu Mari*. The humorous song begins with a daughter asking her mother about possible marriage prospects. In the successive stanzas, the mother runs through the merits of potential husbands, including the fisherman, the butcher, the fruit seller, and the bookkeeper.

I found the Sicilian lyrics in the 1992 edition of "Italian-American Folklore," by Frances M. Malpezzi and William M. Clements. In more recent years, an American audience has been exposed to the folksong, which was used in the wedding scene of Francis Ford Copploa's film, *The Godfather*.

## E LA LUNA MEZZU MARI

E la luna mezzu mari,
Mama mia, mi vogliu maritari.
Figlia mia, cu t'a dari/
Mama mia, penza ci toi.

Si ti dunnu lu pisciaru,
Iddu va, idu veni
Sempri pisci manu teni.
E s'iddu ci piglia la fantasia,
Figlia mia, ti pisculia.

(Chorus)
O mama, pisci fritu e bachala,
O mama, va fatti la fari to!

Si ti dunnu lu carnizzeru,
Iddu va, iddu veni
Sempri salcizza manu teni.
E s'iddu ci piglia la fantasia
Figlia mia, ti salcizzulia.

(Chorus)

Si ti dunnu lu verduleru,
Iddu va, iddu veni
Sempri bonanni manu teni
E s'iddu ci piglia la fantasia,
Figlia mia, ti bonannia.

(Chorus)

Si ti dunnu lu scrivanu,
Iddu va, iddu veni
Sempri lapizzi manu teni
E s'iddu ci piglia la fantasia,
Figlia mia, ti lapizzia.

(Chorus)

Sunday Mass and the Italian Hour segued to the focal event of the week, the family noon time dinner over which my grandfather presided.

The kitchen table, its leaves fully extended, was draped with a pressed white cloth and set with Nana's dinnerware—pale yellow plates and pasta bowls, wreathed in pink roses and edged with a gold scallop. Off to the side was the children's table, where my grandfather's sour red wine was diluted with fizzy ginger ale. His grandchildren were expected to—but did not—enjoy this brush with adulthood.

Cheeks flushed and wearing a fresh calico apron over her Sunday best, Nana was the last to be seated, just as my grandfather was unquestionably the first. She followed the custom of her homeland where country wives were expected to stand and serve their men before taking their seat at the table.

My grandfather poured his nearly opaque homemade wine from a pitcher, releasing its musky oak to the room. As he offered the familiar toast, *Buon Appetito*, short, garnet-hued glasses were raised along with a round of respectful nods in his direction.

Sunday's familiar food ritual remained steadfast, even as *la famiglia* continued to change. The homemade fettuccini, meatballs, and a brimming bowl of sauce were constants, as were thick slices of crusty bread and the *insalata*, a green salad served with tomatoes and onions and simply dressed with olive oil, red wine vinegar, oregano, salt and pepper. Roasted chicken, with an assortment of fresh or canned garden vegetables, was the meat dish most often served to accompany the pasta. On festive occasions, Nana prepared a special pasta, salami, and cheese stuffing for the chicken. On all occasions, she encouraged guests at her table to indulge themselves with the Sicilian definition of hospitality, *"Mangia! Mangia!"* To not rise to the occasion and *Eat! Eat!* was to insult the cook, and no one wanted to risk offending this good woman.

*Carni e pisci, la vita ti crisci.*
YOUR LIFE SPAN INCREASES IF YOU EAT MEAT AND FISH.

## Nana's Sicilian Chicken Stuffing

1/2 pound Tubetini pasta

3 tablespoons olive oil

1/4 pound salami, diced

1 tablespoon parsley

1 clove garlic, chopped

1 egg, lightly beaten

1/4 cup Romano cheese

salt & pepper

Boil the Tubetini in water until al dente. Drain and set aside to cool.

In a medium-size sauté pan, warm the olive oil. Add the salami, parsley, and garlic, stirring over low heat until the flavors are blended.

Combine the beaten egg and Romano cheese in a small bowl. Add it to the salami mixture in the sauté pan, along with the cooked tubetini.

Mix all of the ingredients, season to taste, and cool before stuffing the chicken with it.

*Making a Living...Making a Life*

In my grandparents' home, the production and preparation of food approached sacramental significance and wasting food was thought to be sinful. Nanu's gardens, equivalent to a market garden of today, assured a year round supply of vegetables for the Sunday dinner table while demonstrating his ability to provide for his family—another measure of respectability in the Sicilian community. In addition to the backyard vegetable patch that flourished under Nana's care, my grandfather turned the large, vacant corner lot at the end of Cherry Street into rows of green exactness, with the permission of its owner, Charlie Brown. In 1947, my parents bought the Brown house and the adjacent corner lot where they continued to grow the now extended family's vegetables with my grandparents.

For the entire time that his daughters lived at home, my grandfather planted and maintained a third garden at the home of the Manfredi sisters: Queena, Quibby, Lucy, and Teresa, whose Forrest Street property abutted Charlie Brown's. In exchange for the use of their land, he kept the Manfredis supplied with fresh tomatoes, peppers, onions, garlic, endive, eggplant, fennel, basil, beets, carrots, spinach, fava beans, Swiss chard, and zucchini. The women were the daughters of his deceased friend, Vito Manfredi, who had supported his large family by shining shoes at the Rutland train station. In a show of Sicilian loyalty, my grandfather made sure that his friend's daughters would not go without.

During the years that he worked for the Clarendon-Pittsford Railroad, my grandfather kept a fourth garden on land owned by the railroad, on either side of the tracks, along what is now Ripley Road. The property was made available to company employees as a worker's benefit. Nanu planted potatoes and root crops in the river bottomland that stretched along the banks of Otter Creek, two miles from his home. With inventive necessity, he made a wooden wagon out of grape crates to transport his daughters to work with him and to bring home the produce. Self-reliance was a family affair.

Frank Scafidi worked hard to have a simple life in Vermont. His surviving daughters assure me that "Papa was content in America." Unlike my grandmother, who shed a lifetime of tears for the parents, sisters, and brother with whom she longed to be reunited, my grandfather had no interest in returning to the meager prospects of his homeland. He read the letters addressed to him from his family in private, sealing the news in the locked compartments of his heart. He chose to remember the time he left, when all of Europe was on the move and the young men and women of Sicily were fleeing in droves and in all directions.

In contrast, he loved the liberties that attracted him to his adopted country and the community of "Little Randazzo" that he and his compatriots created in Rutland. Even as I struggle to connect the elegant character in studio portraits with the dutiful laborer bent on fulfilling his dreams, I want to believe that what his daughters tell me is true.

*Francesco Paolo Scafidi on the other side of the Atlantic—
Blue Beach, Quonset Point, Rhode Island.*

## VINO

*Un giorno senza vino e come un giorno senza sole.*
A DAY WITHOUT WINE IS LIKE A DAY WITHOUT THE SUN.

In Rutland, as in Randazzo, the men in the community carried on the annual fall tradition of making a year's supply of *vino*, table wine that was as much a household staple as the daily bread. In the absence of local vineyards, they organized bulk grape purchases which arrived in boxcars from Albany, New York, at the beginning of October. My grandfather's standing order was for "25 cases of red and 25 cases of white." The grapes were delivered to the coal chute side of the house so that he could slide the crates into the cellar where his winemaking operation took place.

The process was straightforward. A hand-turned press, often powered with the help of his daughters, was cemented to the floor in a cordoned-off section near the root cellar. The extracted juices were stored nearby in five wooden barrels for the fermentation period, which included intermittent sampling by his panel of fellow winemakers. My grandfather and his friends did not drink to excess, but they did share the peculiar (in my mind) practice of occasionally dropping a raw egg into their glass of red wine to "build blood."

Once the first barrel was ceremoniously tapped, wine service moved upstairs to the kitchen table, where it was a natural complement to the vegetable, cheese, and pasta dishes in Nana's repertoire. Everyone in the Scafidi family drank a glass of wine with the mid-day and evening meals, in the same way that my generation drank an eight-ounce glass of milk. The old world food custom continued in "Little Randazzo," much to the chagrin of the Sisters of St. Joseph, who intimidated their students with after-lunch breath tests, admonishing them to change their ways. As was often the case, the immigrants' children were caught in the crossfire of conforming or confronting.

*Sicilian Club Picnic, 1940s.*
Front Row, left to right: John Camarda, Anthony Bellomo, Guido Rotella (behind Bellomo), Orlando Lemmo, Joseph Lemmo, Vincent Fucile, Michael LaPiana, Vincent Caggige, John Anzalone, Frank Sofia, and Louis Cala, Jr. Back Row, left to right: Salvatore Anzalone, Salvatore Alfonso, Raymond Caggige, Anthony Sofia, James Magro, Frank Persico, Frank Scafidi, Paul Rizziere, Peter Lemmo, Salvatore Fucile, Richard Abel, Louis Cala, and Art Varga.

## CHAPTER XIX
## SOCIETA' SICULA AMERICANA

*Fuj li cosi tinti, ama li boni, ca 'ntra un mumentu cancianu li sceni.*
AVOID THE BAD, LOVE THE GOOD, BECAUSE THINGS CHANGE IN A MOMENT.

As I traveled through the northeastern region of Sicily where my grandparents' lives began, I experienced many "Ah-ha!" moments. Nothing, however, made a bigger impression on me than observing the solidarity of Sicilian men who cluster on street corners and in public places. Black-capped village elders, their sons, and grandsons gather at the doorsteps of barber, bakery, and butcher shops. They sun themselves in open courtyards, crowd onto benches in shaded piazzas, and shop together at the outdoor markets. All the while they are engaged in simultaneous non-stop conversation—the talking head of a giant octopus, arms rising and falling with the currents.

In the afternoon, they play music, bocce, and card games, breaking away for siestas and evening meals prepared by wives and mothers. After sunset they return to their posts to survey and oversee the village night scene. For Sunday morning Mass, they even squeeze together into pews.

This was the camaraderie that bound my grandfather and his paesani as they gathered under neighborhood street lights in the evening, formed co-ops for bulk food purchases, shared the expense of raising pigs for sausage-making, and coordinated wine grape orders in the fall. At the end of the gardening season, they turned to the outlying woods to hunt rabbit and squirrel with the help of their pet ferrets—always on the lookout for tree and ground mushrooms. Their social and support systems survived the journey from Sicily to Vermont intact.

In Rutland, as in other resettlement communities, new arrivals formed mutual aid societies to provide financial assistance for their members when temporary setbacks, unemployment, or death made it impossible for them to take care of their families.

My grandfather was one of the 23 Charter Members of the *Societa' Sicula Americana, Sicula American Society*, founded June 15, 1927 under the leadership of Antonio Bellomo. The young society was tested the following year when Mariano Rotella, yard foreman for the Columbia Marble finishing company, died after being hit by a large piece of falling marble. Mariano left behind a wife and eight children with no Social Security or pension. The Sicula Society stepped in and made sure that Mariano's family always had enough food and heating fuel.

The brotherhood patterned its organization's governance on the United States federal system of executive, judicial, and legislative powers. The preamble to the *Constitution and By-Laws of the Sicula American Society* states: *The emigrated Sicilians in this great Republic of U.S.A. where a democratic Republic is established; to exercise their duties and to obtain the enjoyment of freedom, constitute a body known as "SICULA AMERICAN SOCIETY."*

The purposes of the Society follow: *to unite all those of Sicilian descent even those of American birth in one great family or branches, loose in this locality and State of Vermont; to educate and to emancipate them to a highly standard of civility without prejudice to their political or religious belief; to make them become citizens of this great Republic of U.S.A.; to defend their will of independence and of liberty; to impose them the respect of all laws that are today in power and all duties that are imposed to all citizens of this Republic, U.S.A.; to pay its member a fee of Ten Dollars weekly effected of sickness or accident after one week of the unlucky happening and to be continued for a period of twelve weeks, if the member has paid its monthly dues of not less than One Dollar, due before the 15$^{th}$ of each month; to pay also a fee of Two Hundred Dollars to the family of a member in case of its eternal departure, that is, death: and a wreath of flowers to the member of wife member in such a case stated above. If a member shall die without a family the Society shall provide for its funeral and shall see that the corpse is well taken care of to its last rest.*

Admission to the society was open to men between the ages of 17 and 50 years who were of good moral standing and physically able, as determined by an examining physician. Active members attended regular meetings, were bound *to obey all deliberation taken by the Society*, and were eligible to vote and hold office. Election of officers (President, Vice-President, Speaker, Financial and Corresponding Secretaries, Treasurer, and three Trustees) was by secret ballot at the first meeting in the month of May. The President's power included nominating a door guard at each meeting.

Honorary membership was conferred by a two-thirds vote of the Society to individuals outside of the group who rendered good service, defined as *cooperating in any way toward moral and material benefit of the Society*. Honorary members did not pay dues or assessments. They were allowed a voice in the Society, but not a vote.

The Society chose *Liberty, Equality, Faith, and Brotherhood* as its motto and the triangle as its emblem. The "tongues" of the Sicula American Society were noted as Italian, Sicilian dialect, and English.

May 1st was recognized as the official annual holiday of the Society, *which shall furnish each year some kind of amusement to divert its members and at the same time to remind them of the date of her birth. Invitations can be made to the member's families and friends to participate in such an affair.*

Keeping alive the social customs and culture of their villages and the old country was also a function of the Society. Rutland's early Sicilians held a holiday party in the winter and an annual picnic at the Clarendon Gorge each summer.

Nana especially enjoyed the picnic, perhaps because it overlapped with her area of expertise—food preparation. In the days leading up to the special event, she literally made bushels of gennets, mussetti, and anise bars to share with others. For her own family, she baked round loaves of bread in the morning, cut them in half while they were still warm, drizzled olive oil over the centers, filling some with anchovies and others with sliced fresh tomatoes and oregano. Homemade cheeses, wine and root beer, a roll of salami, sticks of pepperoni, and an abundance of fresh fruit left no one wanting during a full day of food and fellowship, the staples of a Sicilian holiday.

## THE FEAST

The social centerpiece of the year occurred on or around August 15th, the Feast of the Assumption, with a celebration that mirrors Randazzo's *Festa a La Madonna dell' Assunta,* held at the same time on the other side of the Atlantic. The Catholic holy day marks the body and soul ascension into heaven of the Virgin Mary, Mother of Christ.

In Randazzo, as in all Sicilian villages and cities, at least two types of religious festivals with characteristics unique to the place are held annually. The universally exuberant festivals surrounding the Easter period are explosions of flowers, fireworks, parades, pastries, and the non-stop pealing of church bells. The other lively celebration is held on the feast day of the community's patron or protecting saint.

For at least four centuries, the citizens of Randazzo have renewed their dedication to *Assunta* with a long procession through the city that follows *'a Vara,* a stunning fifty-four foot tall *carro trionfale* (triumphal wagon) with three levels and moving parts. Each year the wagon is bedecked with different fabrics, flowers, and glittering precious metals to add an element of surprise. What evokes the most interest and excitement are the twenty-five children of Randazzo between the ages of ten and twelve who are chosen to represent cheerful little angels on each of the three tiers, giving them greater proximity to the heavens. The young girls and boys are elaborately dressed and literally fastened in place for what is considered to be a privileged experience. Good fortune does come their way as onlookers shower them with sweets and hard candies from house balconies along the parade route. The spectacular event is one of the most renowned of the approximately one thousand *fetas* that take place in Sicily each year.

Beginning in 1933, the sons of Randazzo in Rutland's St. Peter's Church parish did their best to approximate the August 15th feast day celebration they remembered with a processional through the Italian neighborhood, music, fireworks, food, and sometimes a carnival. "The Feast" was held annually for four decades and has had periods of revival since.

The component that I remember best is the procession, for which a life-size statue of the Virgin Mary was draped with a blue silk cape, fastened to a decorated float, and pulled through several streets by men who were honored by their role in the event. Flanking the float were proud-to-be-

*Photo from "Sicilia in Festa," by Sandro Libertino and Daniela Guglielmaci.*

*The 1952 Feast of the Assumption procession en route down Meadow Street. The Sisters of St. Joseph watch from the convent steps; St. Peter's Church is in the background. The photograph, taken by Aldo Merusi, appeared in "The Rutland Herald" on June 19, 1988.*

chosen young girls from the parish wearing white summer dresses, their heads encircled with wreaths of flowers. An Italian marching band and a trailing contingent of fervent parishioners in their Sunday best added merriment and body to the slow-moving-processional. The excitement mounted as the sound of music came closer and closer to our street where we waited, scrubbed and polished for the occasion.

Frequent stops were made at houses along the route to give the occupants a chance to pin dollar bills or jewelry to the Madonna's cape as offerings for her help with their prayerful intentions, or to show gratitude for already answered petitions. A more generous donation reaped an immediate reward for the giver, who was treated to one of the small firework displays that were set off along the procession route. There was no concealing my grandfather's pride as he posted himself on our corner lot, waiting to make his annual contribution that would send a shower of sparklers over his neatly tended vegetable garden and spark a round of applause from the spectators.

*The Scafidi Sisters, left to right:*
*Concetta (Connie), Maria (Mary), Assunta (Alice), and Venera (Veronica).*

# CHAPTER XX
# THE SCAFIDI SISTERS

*Oggo ti, e dumani iu.*
YOUR TURN TODAY, MINE TOMORROW.

This is the story of how the Scafidi girls got their names—a story that I have savored through the years and now return to with fresh insight and renewed appreciation. I imagined this as the first chapter of the family memoir, shedding light on all the rest. To my surprise, it is the last.

## VENERA

Francesco and Antonia followed Sicilian tradition and named their first child, born five months after their emigration, in honor of Francesco's mother, Venera Arcey Scafidi of Randazzo. The Italian name, which appears on Venera's birth certificate, means "pious one, the woman who venerates." In the baptismal registry of St. Peter's Church, recorded less than one month after the child's birth, Venera is crossed out in favor of the Catholic saint's name, Veronica, which is written above it. Unaware of the change, her parents continued to call their eldest daughter Venera for all of their lives. When she went to school, the teaching nuns

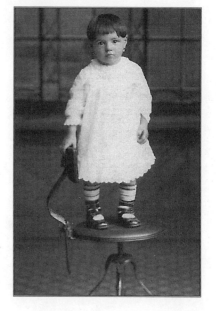

chose to refer to her as Veronica. At her confirmation, she took the feminine version of her father's Anglicized name, Frances, for the middle name her parents did not give her. Perhaps in confusion, or to avoid conflict, her sisters simply called her "Vi" (pronounced "Vee"), a name that stuck until she entered the business world where her co-workers called her Ronny. Her husband and all of the acquaintances she made following her marriage were introduced to her as Ronny. So strong was her association with the final rendition of her name, that she considered her fourth child, Ronald Francis, to be her namesake. To her nieces and nephews, she was Aunt Vi. When she retired, Veronica volunteered in a Foster Grandparent program. For fifteen years, she worked side by side with the Sisters of St. Joseph as a teaching assistant in Rutland's remaining parochial school, Christ the King. On the day of her funeral, April 3, 1996, the entire student body marched from the "Irish" school on the other side of the city to fill the pews of St. Peter's Church, in honor of the devoted woman they knew as Grandma Ronny.

*Venera Scafidi and Helen Sangra on their First Holy Communion Day.*

*Venera and her Confirmation Sponsor, Commari Domenica Cotrupi.*

## CONCETTA

Tradition was also considered in the name of the couple's second child, born less than one year later. Maria Concetta was named in honor of Antonia's mother, Concetta Citra Delpopolo of Castiglione di Sicilia. Dr. Powers, who signed her birth certificate, could have easily interpreted the soft Sicilian "c" before the vowel "e" as a "g," since he listed her name as Maria Congetta. In St. Peter's baptismal registry, her first name is recorded as Concetta, without mention of Maria, or a middle name. When her parents said Concetta, in their rapid Sicilian dialect, it sounded like Conjata to her nieces and nephews who shortened the name to Aunt Jata. Her sisters used the even more abbreviated Ci. In school, she was known as Concetta. In the workplace, outside of the Italian community, to her husband and the new friends she made later in life, she was Connie.

*Maria, Venera, and Concetta Scafidi.*

## MARIA

The third daughter, born two years later, was named after Antonia's closest sister in age, Maria Delpopolo of Catania, Sicily. The child's birth certificate gives her full name as Mary Scafidi, while her baptismal record lists Maria. She also gave herself a middle name when confirmed. Believing that she was taking her mother's first name, she chose Antoinette. Her teachers and school friends called her Mary. Her parents continued to say Maria, but it sounded like "Madia." Now, one might think that the straightforward Maria/Mary would provide little room for an appellation detour. Not so. Her sisters called her Mae, a name that expanded to Mamie, which took her through the years of work and marriage, putting her in the good company of popular First Lady Mamie Eisenhower.

## ASSUNTA

The baby of the family, as she was referred to well into her adult life, was born three years later on August 15th, the feast day of Randazzo's Madonna dell' Assunta, Rutland's Feast of the Assumption. Her parents made a clear decision to honor their Catholic and Sicilian roots in naming their fourth daughter Assunta. The name stands alone on her baptismal record, registered three months after her birth. Her birth certificate, however, shows Assumpta (perhaps, as in Assumption?) as her middle name, and Alice (!!!) as her first. Someone's attempt to Anglicize Assunta with Alice Assumpta defies further explanation. To complicate matters, her sisters called her Sue, the name she always used to introduce herself. In school, and on all official documents, she was Alice. Picking up on the dialectic sound of her name, Assunda, her nieces and nephews conferred yet another moniker, Aunt Sunda.

Applying today's pop psychology, it seems safe to say that the Scafidi Sisters were entitled to an identity crisis—if not for the multiplicity of names, then for the divided worlds they straddled as first generation Italian-Americans. At every turn of their lives they faced the uncharted waters with sets of opposing directions. They learned to rely on each other for the understanding and support that their parents, the staunch supporters and enforcers of tradition, were unable to give them.

Their small circle of familial intimacy was slightly enlarged, but not much altered, by their *compari* and *commari*, the sponsors their mother and father chose to stand by them in Baptism and Confirmation. These Sicilian family friends were afforded special respect and always addressed with their title, as in the case of Compari and Commari Foti, who stood up for Concetta at her baptism, and Commari Cotrupi, Venera's confirmation sponsor. The families often shared holiday celebrations and the girls and their assigned compari and commari exchanged Easter and Christmas gifts—home deliveries of their mother's pastries for bags of hard candy.

The girls adored their "Papa" and were devoted to "Mama," who gave birth to all of them at home. Not long after their proud father sent notice of a newborn to families in Sicily, a homemade baby blanket with a tiny gold ring and a pair of matching earrings hidden in the hand-stitched binding arrived in the mail. Their mother responded by following the custom of piercing her infant daughter's ears.

Growing up, the sisters were paired in two bedrooms—Venera with Maria and Concetta with Assunta, encouraging special bonds that would last a lifetime. The younger two were very close to their mother, while Venera and Concetta were given more of their father's attention, not always to their advantage. The once adventurous young man who braved an ocean between himself and his parents, embracing all that America had to offer, applied rigid rules of a patriarchal culture to his daughters' every attempt at independence. The double standard was all that he knew, and family loyalty, which translated to obedience and respect for the head of the household, was what his daughters understood. In all things, Papa was The Boss.

He was as indulgent as he was strict. It was Papa who started the girls on forays beyond home and school to places their mother did not venture. Forever mindful of appearance for appearance's sake (presenting a *bella figura*, beautiful image, to the outside world), he lined them up for inspection before leaving the house. If someone or something did not meet with his approval, it fell to his wife to fix the problem, or the discordant daughter would be left behind.

He took the girls shopping for the one good pair of shoes he insisted they have every year. The shoes had to be "Buster Browns" and the purchases had to be made at the New York Clothing Store on West Street. He was his daughters' fashion barometer and coordinator. He gave them their haircuts and chose family portrait dresses that were handed down and down, as well as the few articles of clothing that supplemented their homemade wardrobes.

*The Scafidi Sisters*

Starting with the eldest, he took one girl at a time to ten-cent Saturday matinees starring his cowboy heroes, Tom Mix and Gene Autrey. He took great pleasure in these outings, as he once had in attending Randazzo's famed puppet theaters where nearly life-size English knights clashed swords in weekly dramas that whetted his boyhood appetite for adventure.

On Christmas Eve, he helped his daughters hang four of his worn and discarded rag wool work socks by the kitchen stove with the hopes that St. Nicholas would visit during the night. He filled them with chestnuts to roast on Christmas Day, hard-to-find prickly pears whose bushes sprawl across Sicily, an orange and a pomegranate, Hershey Kisses and Nonpareils. He was also known to leave a stocking full of coal for a daughter he felt less deserving. "That was O.K.," says Aunt Jata. "Papa was just trying to teach us a lesson."

Papa had a strong sense of what was appropriate conduct for his daughters, as well as what was disgracefully American. High on that list was a girl playing sports.

In my mother's 1939 high school yearbook, the caption under her photo reads, "Vi is a grand basketball center." She was a member of the Athletic Association for all of her years at the Academy. Not only was she "a flash on the court" during her four years on the school's first all-girls basketball team, she was captain! "Vi never missed a game; she possesses more than her share of school spirit. She's out for success and fame!" the caption continues.

How did she manage? With classic Sicilian secretiveness—and the help of her sisters, who inventively covered for her absences during practices and games, stealthily lowering her out the bedroom window when necessary. Mae babysat a gaggle of Cotrupi children and Ci did housework for the Mandredi family to make installment payments on the suede varsity jacket and duffle bag their older sister needed to be on the team. They furtively delivered their 25-cent earnings to Wilson's Sports, whittling down their substantial debt in a grand conspiracy against their parents, who remained in the dark.

There were bigger challenges ahead, not as easily overcome.

VENERA

At the age of 19, Venera's attempt to join high school friends who had landed newly available high-paying government jobs for women in Washington D.C. was promptly squelched by her father. After insisting that she work in Rutland, live at home, and contribute to the family income until she found a husband, he tried to cement his plan by arranging her marriage to the son of a Sicilian friend.

When I was a young girl, I discovered journals in which my mother made intermittent entries during the years of yearning between high school and marriage. They reveal a thoroughly romantic young woman, who loved to read sequestered in her room after work, devouring book after book. In the fall she enjoyed shuffling through the dried leaves in evening walks around the city, particularly when it rained and she could carry an umbrella and cinch her *London Fog* raincoat tightly around her. One summer she converted her father's shed into a sewing room and made herself twenty-five gabardine suits with the latest Vogue patterns. The woman who loved fashion and color vowed to enter the convent at age 25 if she had not found a suitable husband. Months shy of the self-imposed deadline, her lucky stars delivered an equally sentimental suitor who took her for moonlight rides in the countryside singing *You Are My Sunshine*. He was neither Italian nor Catholic, but Hungarian and Methodist. In his own time, my grandfather accepted his first son-in-law, Arthur Varga, and even sponsored him as a member of the Sicula Society.

# Autographs

Sister Mary Annunciata, S.S.J.
Sr. Mary Jerome
Sr. Francis Marie
Sr. Jane Frances
Sister M. Evangelist
Rev. J. D. Sullivan
Rev. T. H. Connor
Sr. M. Bernadette
Mother M. Josephine
Sr. M. Imelda
God Bless Veronica
Sr. M. Loretto
Sr. M. Frances
Sr. M. Felicitas
Sr. Mary Matthew
Sr. Mary Concepta
Sr. M. Eucharia
O. J. Baldwin
Sr. Mary Clementine

*Venera's high school yearbook photo with autographs by the Sisters of St. Joseph.*

*Venera in one of the hand-knit sweaters
in which she outfitted her family over the years.*

*Coming of age in the World War II years.*

*Arthur and Veronica Scafidi Varga on their honeymoon in New York City, November 1945. They stayed at the Hotel New Yorker at 34th Street and 8th Avenue.*

## CONCETTA

Concetta's repeated pleas to become a nurse were met with complete resistance by her father who regarded the notion of his daughter caring for strange men with contempt. "In Italy, men care for men, and women care for women." Aspirations crushed, Concetta took her considerable sewing skills to the nearby Dick's Dress Shop where "floor lady," Rose Delotoso, started her off attaching sleeves and collars to the piecework bundles of twelve that passed through her work station. Arthur Dick, who inherited the business from his father, and one machinist who repaired the equipment, were the only men in the three-floor building with a pecking order of 125 women pattern cutters, sewers, thread clippers, pressers, and inspectors.

Concetta lived at home and worked at the dress factory for the next thirteen years until she married a man who was also outside the Italian community. Up to that time, she turned over all but 25-cents of her weekly paycheck to Papa, from whom she subsequently had to ask for spending money. Eventually, Concetta's husband, Bill Miglis, shared enough common interests with his father-in-law to forge a fine friendship. When the couple moved into my grandparents' upstairs apartment, their son Billy quickly became the apple of Papa's eye. At last, he had the son he made no secret of having always wanted.

*Concetta poses with her parents on her wedding day, June 28, 1952.*

*Bill Miglis while on honeymoon, Hampton Beach, New Hampshire.*

*Concetta and her son, Billy, in front of her parents' house with Cherry Street in the background, 1954.*

## MARIA

Two weeks after her high school graduation, Maria's dentist, Dr. Baptista Chiolino, who was new to the area, offered her a job as his dental assistant. The salary was $10 a week without benefits. Maria Zambone, who was still living in the upstairs apartment of the family house, was delighted to make her former sewing student fashionable white uniforms embellished with intricate detail. In no time, Dr. Chiolino offered to cover all of Maria's expenses for her to attend Tufts University's dental hygienist program. Recalling the futile attempts of her older sisters to expand their horizons, daughter number three decided not to confront her father about a move to Boston.

Maria lived at home for the next ten years, keeping her dental assistant job and buckling to Papa's opinion of the young men she dated. She cut off a serious relationship with a tall, blonde police officer of German descent when her father threatened to have nothing to do with her for the rest of her life if she married "the foreigner." On the contrary, he heartily approved of Chief Petty Officer Emanuel Valleroli who became re-acquainted with Maria while home on leave and asked her to marry him. "Nanny" who emigrated from Gela, Sicily with his mother when he was six years old, was a familiar and accepted member of the Italian community.

*Sue and Mamie leaving for vacation—destination, Lake George, New York.*

*Vi and Mamie—best friends forever.*

*Chief Torpedoman Emanuel S. Valleroli,
retired as Chief Petty Officer after 23 years of service with the U.S. Navy.*

*Mamie sketched her wedding gown for a seamstress at Rutland's Vogue Shoppe.*

*Mr. and Mrs. Emanuel Valleroli leave for their honeymoon in Washington, D.C.*

## ASSUNTA

Assunta also married a good Italian man from the other side of the Strait of Messina. Her sister, Mary, introduced her to Almerico Cioffi, the younger brother of Alberico, who Mary had dated for awhile. It helped that "Al" had worked with Papa at Howe Scale before serving with the 121st Seabee Battalion of the U.S. Navy during World War II. While overseas, he mailed his mother a diamond engagement ring which he asked her to bring, with his proposal of marriage, to his girlfriend, Sue Scafidi—and her father, Francesco.

My fondest memories of Aunt Sunda are of the glamorous career girl, who painted her fingernails firehouse red and turned heads with her clotheshorse wardrobe, all-occasion silk scarves, and an eye-popping collection of costume jewelry. She was the fearless family prankster and master joke-teller who challenged her father with what he perceived to be a lack of feminine decorum. Occasionally, when Papa was not around, she would dare to smoke a cigarette with her cup of coffee, pursing her red lips to blow practiced circles of smoke into the air.

She, too, lived at home, working as a secretary and bank teller before marrying at 25. Every Wednesday, just as in the ads for *Prince Spaghetti Night*, she and Al joined his extended Napolitano family for one of Ma Cioffi's Italian dinners.

*Sue during her engagement years, 1949-1952.*

*U.S. Navy Seabee Al Cioffi.*

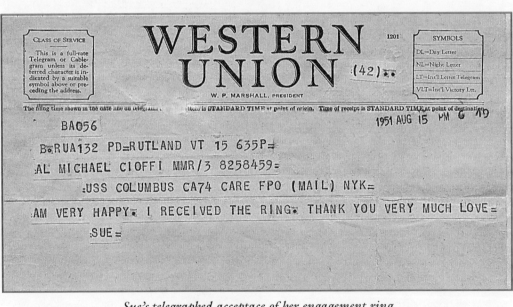

*Sue's telegraphed acceptace of her engagement ring,
dated August 15, 1951, her 24th birthday.*

The Scafidi sisters did not devote any time to talking about what might have been in their lives. Nor did they express resentment for their father's heavy-handed interference. On the contrary, in the religion of their sisterhood they spoke of Papa in reverential terms.

*Papa surrounded by his daughters on Maria's wedding day, April 16, 1951, when he was too ill to give the bride away. Front row: Francesco, Judy Varga, Antonia, Sandy Varga. Back Row: Assunta, Concetta, Maria and Emanuel Valleroli, Arthur (who accompanied the bride to the altar) and Veronica Varga.*

My grandmother, who had fulfilled my every home-away-from-home need with a seat at her kitchen table and an occasional tear of understanding, was not able to prepare her daughters for a world in which she did not participate. The sisters' stories of the confusion and embarrassment that pervaded their young lives were airbrushed with a little more humor at each retelling. The predictable punch line was, "We didn't know!"

Through all the years of their lives the four sisters' primary identity continued to be with each other. That was made abundantly clear to their families and to the greater Italian community, whose members perhaps understood the sisters better than the sisters' husbands and children could.

It was not as individuals, but as the Scafidi Sisters that they gave gifts and signed birthday, wedding, sympathy, and Mass cards. They called each other and their mother frequently throughout the day, speaking exclusively in the family dialect "lest the walls and wires" be privy to their conversations. They met for coffee at Nana's kitchen table in the morning, and sometimes in the afternoons, locking heads in rapid Sicilian conversations that excluded all others who did not understand the language. They confided their dreams from the night before, seeking Nana's interpretation of their meaning and significance. In the summer they sipped Schweppes's Ginger Ale while listening to their beloved Red Sox games on the radio. They cherished and looked out for each other's children as though they were their own, sharing wholeheartedly in all the details of their lives, giving before being asked.

There was a comfortable sense of knowing among these four women. Their laughter never seemed heartier than when shared with one another and the tears of any one sister triggered "the good cry they all needed anyway." Whatever conflict they felt in their relationships remained below the surface, sparing them the scars so many siblings inflict upon one another.

Their Catholic faith and collective resignation to Divine will sustained them as it had their Sicilian ancestors. All through their school years and in all kinds of weather, Venera and Maria attended early morning Mass at the Sisters of St. Joseph's convent chapel. In their adult years, all four met in "their" pew every Sunday for 6 o'clock Mass at St. Peter's Church. The surviving sister, Aunt Mamie Valleroli, now in their mid-80s and living with one of her daughters near the Naval Base in Virginia Beach, continues the tradition of "saying the rosary" every night before bed. She recently confided that when she closes her eyes to start the string of *Hail Marys*, in her mind she is kneeling with Vi, to the right of the altar in the convent chapel "at home."

## SHIRLEY

As the oldest grandchild, I enjoyed early admittance to the Scafidi Sisters' inner circle. It helped that I cracked the code of their mother's dialect at the same time I was learning to speak English. Consequently, I was treated to many of the recycled one-for-all and all-for-one childhood stories they shared around whatever kitchen table they gathered. My favorite story features a porcelain doll with a delicately sculpted face, blonde ringlets, and blue eyes named Shirley.

*The Scafidi Sisters*

The summer I was nine years old, I screwed up enough courage to enter the Meadow Street Playground's annual Doll Contest. The problem was, which of my dolls to bring? Should I compete in the Baby Doll category? In the Bride Doll category? In the Most Beautiful? Thanks to my mother and Santa Claus, I had them all.

I took my dilemma to the sisters' morning klatch. Almost immediately, first one, then the other shouted, "Vi, go get your doll!"

"Mom has a doll?" I asked in near disbelief.

After a considerable amount of prodding, my mother left the room, returning with an old shoebox held together with store twine. She placed it in the center of the table with the big sister air of, "There, now are you satisfied?"

Off came the cover and up on their toes went my three aunts, clucking, cooing and craning for a look. Very gently, a pretty smiling doll, wearing a pleated pink organdy dress and white kid leather shoes, albeit out of date, was lifted out and passed around.

"Oh Vi, remember how you hugged her and talked to her?" said a misty-eyed Aunt Jata. "Oh, how you loved her!"

"Your mother never let the rest of us touch her," Aunt Sunda chimed in. "She hid the doll under her bed or in Papa's shed where we wouldn't find her."

One severe winter while the doll was stored in Papa's shed, the cold sent two cracks down her composition face. I was startled, but no one else seemed to mind. They all had a stake in this vintage 1936, 17-inch replica of Shirley Temple, the child actor who enjoyed enormous popularity in the 1930s. She was the most photographed celebrity of the time which drove millions of her childhood fans to buy Shirley dolls.

At the age of 15, my mother was one of those devotees who eagerly awaited each of the little starlet's new movies—and, she really wanted a doll. There was never enough money in the Scafidi household to buy frivolous things, no less a doll during the Depression years. But then my mother saw a magazine ad for *White Cloverine Brand Salve* which offered Shirley Temple dolls and bicycles as premiums for girls and boys willing to make door-to-door sales. She convinced her three younger sisters to canvas the neighborhood, on her behalf, promoting 25-cent containers of the all-purpose salve to friends and neighbors.

I cannot imagine how many one-ounce tins it took to earn the "Baby Take A Bow" doll named for the song and dance routine that launched Shirley Temple's acting career. As always, her sisters came through for her and now they wanted to help me. One by one they offered assurances that the judges would be blown away. This doll defied all categories! Eventually even I was convinced and, that very afternoon, off to the playground the fairly fragile Shirley and I went.

The judges asked all of the contestants—there were probably 30 to 40 of us—to stand in a circle, holding dolls at chest height, facing center. Then they proceeded to walk around the ring, commenting and asking friendly questions. I could barely repress my excitement as the three judges made their way toward Shirley and me. I am still not certain if I saw one of them wince when I confidently declared my competition category as "Best of Show."

Unless you count the sympathetic looks from some of the other contenders, it's probably not a surprise to learn that Shirley and I did not win a prize nor an honorable mention. Of course, the Scafidi sisters' take on it was that the judges just didn't get it. They couldn't recognize a rare and valuable collectible even when it was right in front of their eyes.

After that thwarted return to celebrity, "Baby Take A Bow" went back in the box to her hiding place. From time to time something would trigger the memory of her and I would ask my mother what she planned to do with the doll. As the years went by I began to feel a sentimental attachment to Shirley. My mother seemed nonplussed by my interest, which led me to believe that the doll was more meaningful to her than I had imagined.

Fast forward to Christmas 1995, the last I spent with my mother although at the time there was no reason for either of us to suspect that it would be. I was a widow of one year, but she had been living alone since 1973. An hour's drive over the mountain that separated our Vermont valleys was easy and my visits to her were frequent. (My mother never learned to drive.) We both looked forward to our long-standing holiday tradition of going out to dinner after having a private gift exchange under her tree.

That year my mother had two gifts waiting for me—one fetchingly wrapped in a large dress box that begged to be opened first. Inside was a beautiful, white on white, queen-size quilt with intricate designs created by her perfect tiny stitches. It was a reproduction of an antique quilt pattern that I had long admired and she had secretly worked on it all year. The gift was so overwhelming that I had to be reminded of the smaller package.

I recognized the old shoebox inside the wrap immediately. Forty years after the infamous doll show, my mother had decided to pass along "Baby Take A Bow" to me! I was so moved by the sweetness of the moment that all I could say was, 'Oh, thank you, Mom."

"I suppose you'll want to keep her under one of those glass domes," said my mother with her inherited Sicilian stoicism.

"Don't worry, Mom," I answered. "You know I'll take good care of her. I promise."

*Francesco and Antonia in their back yard on Cherry Street.*

# EPILOGUE

*Supra lu majuri si 'nsigna lu minùri.*
WE LEARN BY STANDING ON THE SHOULDERS OF THE WISE.

Nana lived long enough to knit tiny sweaters for my two children, Stephen and Heather. They, in turn, have children who call me "Nana." I am delighted to hear that familiar word in the young voices of Rhaine, Tully, Alex, and Cassie—names that would sound foreign to Francesco Paolo and Antonia Maria Scafidi.

Ethnicity is not a defining characteristic for this fifth generation of Italian, Spanish, Hungarian, English, Irish, Scottish, French, and Abenaki ancestry. The boundless opportunities of their time will provide a different set of challenges than those that beckoned and constrained previous generations.

The extended family of Francesco and Antonia Scafidi now approaches fifty. It sprawls across the country and includes educators, engineers, doctors, artists, scientists, and business professionals, as well as two nurses and a dental hygienist. Whenever and wherever we gather, we raise our glasses to recall the spirit of generosity, loyalty, and love of family that unites us—the legacy of Francesco and Antonia. I think that these intrepid travelers would be pleased to join us in celebration of the journey they started.

*A la Famiglia!*

## Black Dresses
### by Maria Mazziotti Gillan

*I dress now all in black like the old ladies*
*of my childhood, the old ladies who watched*

*our movements and reported to our mothers*
*if we did anything wrong. These women, sitting*

*on their stoops in their shiny black cotton, their black*
*stockings rolled down to just below their knees,*

*their sparse, white hair drawn back into a bun, wisps*
*of it escaping onto their foreheads.*

*In the heat of an August afternoon, they sat and fanned*
*themselves with accordion fans that they held*

*in their hands and moved back and forth to create*
*some movement of air. They had big white cotton*

*handkerchiefs they used to pat away the sweat.*
*These women kept their eyes on the neighborhood.*

*They could have told all the secrets of each house,*
*and on evenings, late, sitting under the grape arbor,*

*while the men played briscole and the children sat quietly,*
*they told the secrets whispered among the women,*

*the secrets they held close to them, these women*
*who were always there for one another.*

*When there was illness in the family, they would come*
*to the door with pots of soup and fresh bread, ready*

*to help clean the floors or care for the children.*
*Summer evenings under the grape arbor, the children heard*

*those stories and they stored them in their hearts,*
*and the women's whispers and laughter became*

*the music of a time when the world was small*
*enough to carry in their hands.*

# FAMILY
# GENEALOGY

*November 24, 1945. Andrew and Esther Varga, Arthur Varga, Veronica Scafidi Varga, Mary Scafidi, George Varga, Antonia and Frank Scafidi.*

# THE FAMILY GENEALOGY

## VENERA

Venera *Veronica Frances* Scafidi, born 9 March 1921 in Rutland, Vermont; married 24 November 1945 at St. Peter's Church in Rutland, Vermont, to Arthur Robert Varga of Chittenden, Vermont, born 8 December 1923, son of Andras Lajos *Andrew Louis* and Ezster *Esther* (Tarsci) Varga of Chittenden, Vermont.

Veronica (Scafidi) and Arthur Varga had five children, including: Sandra Marie, Judith Antoinette, Robert Arthur, Ronald Francis, and Arthur Robert, Jr. Veronica and Arthur Varga divorced 5 November 1974. Veronica died 31 March 1996 at 75 years. Arthur died 14 July 2009 at 85 years.

Arthur's father, Andras Lajos Varga, was born 31 December 1881 in Bihar County of the Kingdom of Hungary, the son of Sandor *Alexander* and Marie (Dame) Varga, also of Bihar County. On 4 November 1903, Andras married Ezster Tarsci, born 14 March 1887 in Bihar County, daughter of Lajos *Louis* Tarsci and Ezster *Esther* (Bake )Tarsci of Bihar County. In 1904, Andras emigrated to the United States where he traveled for a year in search of a place to settle. After deciding on New Haven, Vermont, he sent for his wife, Ezster, who sold her husband's wheelwright business in Bahir County and crossed the Atlantic alone to join him. Andras and Ezster later purchased a large farm in Chittenden, Vermont and had eight children, including: Yolan *Mary*, Irene, Emma, Christine, Andrew, Arthur, George, and Aranka. Andras died in Rutland, Vermont 27 December 1962 at 81 years. Ezster also died in Rutland 6 March 1968 at 81 years.

### Venera (Veronica Frances) Scafidi & Arthur Robert Varga

A. Sandra Marie Varga  
   b. 18 September 1946  
   m. 4 February 1967  

   Philip Dodge Levesque  
   b. 4 July 1938  
   d. 15 July 1994 at 56 years  

   i. Stephen Philip Levesque  
      b. 19 June 1969  
      m. 6 August 1994  

      Mari Kathryn Brennan  
      b. 28 April 1967  

      a. Rhaine Brennan Levesque  
         b. 7 November 1996  

      b. Alexander Philip Levesque  
         b. 10 August 1999  

   ii. Heather Judith Levesque  
       b. 1 November 1970  
       m. 7 June 1997  

       Matthew Paul Goldrick  
       b. 18 September 1970  

       a. Tully Luke Goldrick  
          b. 30 November 1998  

       b. Cassandra Marie Goldrick  
          b. 13 June 2004  

B. Judith Antoinette Varga  
   b. 24 January 1949  
   m. 27 June 1976  

   Victor Henry Lamberti  
   b. 9 July 1946  

   i. Anna Veronica Lamberti  
      b. 23 August 1981  
      d. 21 December 1992 at 11 years  

   ii. Victor Anthony Lamberti II  
       b. 30 April 1986

C.  Robert Arthur Varga          Lucinda Baker Kurant
    b. 24 December 1950          b. 1 February 1948
    m. 25 March 1995

    1.  Jason Alec Kurant
        b. 11 April 1967

    2.  Sabrina Anne Kurant      Lawrence DeForest Provost III
        b. 15 April 1969         b. 20 October 1971
        m. 17 May 1997

        a.  Cameron Lawrence Provost
            b. 8 May 2002

        b.  Kierstin Baker Provost
            b. 16 July 2005

    3.  Jennifer Louise Kurant
        b. 3 December 1970

D.  Ronald Francis Varga         Pamela Kay Duff
    b. 4 September 1954          b. 23 April 1955
    m. 24 June 1977

    i.  Bethany Ann Varga        Sylvester Winfred Owusu
        b. 12 November 1979      b. 5 November 1981
        m. 21 October 2006

    ii. Sara Michele Varga       Michael Joe Earnest, Jr.
        b. 16 December 1981      b. 12 March 1978
        m. 17 September 2008

        a.  Alina Jule Varga
            b. 5 April 2000

E.  Arthur Robert Varga, Jr.     Lorilynn Moore
    b. 2 December 1955           b. 7 October 1959
    m. 3 January 1981
    div. 27 January 1985

*June 28, 1952. Front row: Alice Miglis, Flower Girl Sandra Varga, and Irene Miglis. Back row; Arthur Varga, John Miglis, William Miglis, Concetta Scafidi Miglis, Alice Cioffi, and Robert Densmore.*

## CONCETTA

Maria Concetta *Connie* Scafidi, born 16 December 1922 in Rutland, Vermont; married 28 June 1952 at St. Peter's Church in Rutland, Vermont, to William Matthew Miglis of Center Rutland, Vermont, born 24 May, 1924 in Florence, Vermont, son of Frank Miglis, born 4 October 1894 in Czechoslavakia, and Mary (Plisko) Miglis, born 23 May 1899 in Scranton, Pennsylvania, of Center Rutland, Vermont. Concetta (Scafidi) and William Miglis had one son, William Paul. Concetta died 16 June 2009 at 86 years.

William Matthews' father, Frank, worked in the marble quarries of Florence and West Rutland, as well as in the slate quarries of West Pawlett. During the years of Frank's employment, the Miglis family lived in Florence, West Pawlett, and Rutland before settling in Center Rutland. William and Mary (Plisko) Miglis had eight children, including: George, Mary, Pauline, William, Frank, Irene, Alice, and John. Frank Miglis died 4 October 1992 at 98 years; Mary (Plisko) Miglis died 31 March 1993 at 94 years.

### Maria Concetta (Connie) Scafidi & William Matthew Miglis

A.     William Paul Miglis        Karen Elizabeth Manley (1)
       b. 29 December 1953        b. 1 September 1953
       m. 23 March 1974 (1)
       div. 1987
       m. 18 August 1990 (2)

                                         Brenda Ann Combatti (2)
                                         b.14 December 1952

      i.     Jennifer Elizabeth Miglis     Matthew Edward Pitts
             b. 9 July 1979                     b. 22 December 1975
             m. 11 August 2006

           a.     Tyler Austin Pitts
                 b. 1 January 1998

           b.     Cayden Thomas Pitts
                 b. 13 August 2007

      ii.    Adam Matthew Miglis
             b. 7 February 1986

*April 16, 1951. Arthur Varga, Mary Scafidi Valleroli, Emanuel Valleroli, Concetta Miglis, and Phillip Valleroli.*

# MARIA

Maria *Mary* Scafidi, born 8 July 1924 in Rutland, Vermont; married 16 April 1951, at St. Peter's Church in Rutland, Vermont, to Emanuel Salvatore Valleroli of Rutland, Vermont, born 5 November 1919 in Gela, Italy, son of Francesco and Rosaria (Garrasi) Valleroli of Rutland, Vermont.

Maria (Scafidi) and Emanuel Valleroli had three children, including twin girls, Charron Marie and Susan Marie, born eleven minutes apart on December 9 and 10, and another daughter, Frances Rosaria. Emanuel Valleroli died 30 December 1990 in Norfolk, Virginia at 71 years.

Emanuel's father, Francesco Valleroli, was born 13 August 1889 in Gela, Sicily. Rosaria (Garrasi) Valleroli was also born in Gela, 8 April 1892. Francesco was 23 years old and married when he first emigrated, without Rosaria, to the United States in search of work. He arrived at Ellis Island on 8 October 1912 aboard the passenger ship, Anocona, from the port of Palermo, Sicily. Francesco was a "bird of passage," criss-crossing the Atlantic from Gela to Rutland several times before permanently settling in Rutland. Rosaria did not join him there until 1925, when she emigrated with their two sons, eight-year-old Philip and six-year-old Emanuel. The couple's three other children, Phillip, Concetta, and Agatha, died from an outbreak of plague in Sicily. Francesco and Rosaria had four more children, all born in Rutland. They include Ettore, Grace, Angelo, and Sadie. Angelo died at two years. Rosaria died 18 October 1953 in Rutland, Vermont at 61 years. Francesco also died in Rutland on 9 January 1972 at 83 years.

### Maria (Mary) Scafidi & Emanuel Salvatore Valleroli

A.  Charron Marie Valleroli
    b. 9 December 1951

B.  Susan Marie Valleroli                Andrew Arthur Brock
    b. 10 December 1951                  b. 2 September 1952
    m. 22 November 1975

    i.  Charron Jennifer Brock           Brandon Matthew Bosch
        b. 16 March 1981                 b. 28 December 1980
        m. 5 October 2008

ii. Courtney Andrea Brock
b. 1 October 1988

C. Frances Rosaria Valleroli      Montford Erlon Oakes
b. 5 April 1955      b. 20 April 1953
m. 13 October 1990

*December 6, 1952. Front row: Flower Girls Judith Varga and Benadette Cioffi. Back row: Theodore Kramarz, Alberico Cioffi, Almerigo Cioffi, Alice Scafidi Cioffi, Mary Lemmo, and Bernard Lawrence.*

# ASSUNTA

Alice Assunta *Sue* Scafidi, born 15 August 1927 in Rutland, Vermont; married 6 December 1952 at St. Peter's Church in Rutland, Vermont, to Almerigo *Al* Michael Cioffi of Rutland, Vermont, born 29 April 1926 in Rutland, Vermont, son of Mariano Michele and Benadette (Ruggiero) Cioffi of Rutland, Vermont. Alice Assunta died 22 October 2004 in Rutland, Vermont at 77 years. Almerigo Cioffi also died in Rutland on 16 January 2008 at 82 years. Alice Assunta (Scafidi) and Almerigo Cioffi had two daughters, Michele Antoinette and Joanne Marie.

Almerigo's father, Mariano Michele Cioffi, born 28 January 1889 in Cervinara, Italy, married Benadette (Ruggiero), born 22 June 1894 in Cervinara, on 2 October 1919 in Cervinara. In 1905, at the age of 16, Mariano and his brother, Ralph, emigrated to the United States. Mariano returned to Italy and married Benadette. Following their wedding in 1919, the couple emigrated to Rutland, Vermont. Mariano and Benadette had four children, all born in Rutland. They include Ralph, Alberico, Almerigo, and Louise. Mariano died 21 June 1959 in Rutland, Vermont at 71 years. Benadette also died in Rutland on 7 February 1993 at 74 years.

### Alice Assunta (Sue) Cioffi & Almerigo (Al) Michele Cioffi

A.  Michele Antoinette Cioffi  William Charles Belmonte
    b. 6 April 1957  b. 21 March 1962
    m. 2 April 2000

B.  Joanne Marie Cioffi  Peter Adrian Louras
    b. 11 February 1961  b. 15 April 1960
    m. 21 September 1985

    i.  Emily Michele Louras
        b. 20 December 1991

## ABOUT THE AUTHOR

Sandra Levesque, of Randolph, Vermont, is a marketing/public relations consultant who combines her interest in history and storytelling in this three generation memoir. Starting in the late 19th century, the author traces her maternal family from the Etna region of Sicily's mountainous interior to the northern reaches of New England in Rutland, Vermont, the historical center of the state's marble industry.

Made in the USA
Charleston, SC
09 September 2011